Follow Me: BE HUMAN

Follow Me: BE
HUMAN

by GEORGE H. SALLAWAY

Helicon • Baltimore-Dublin

Helicon Press, Inc.
1120 N. Calvert Street
Baltimore, Maryland 21202

Helicon Limited
20 Upr. Fitzwilliam St.
Dublin 2, Ireland

Library of Congress Catalog Card Number 66-17081

Nihil Obstat: Carroll E. Satterfield
Censor Librorum

Imprimatur: ✠ Lawrence Cardinal Shehan
Archbishop of Baltimore
May 18, 1966

PRINTED IN THE UNITED STATES OF AMERICA BY
GARAMOND/PRIDEMARK PRESS, BALTIMORE, MARYLAND

to my mother

"the Christe'd beauty of her mind
her mold of features mated well."

G. M. HOPKINS

Preface

THIS BOOK WAS WRITTEN BECAUSE I DIDN'T LIKE THE VIRTUES. I suspect this is not an uncommon state among those of us who have been exposed to the customary presentation. I, for one, dutifully attended to all the categories and sub-categories invented to contain these free-flowing energies of the Christian life. I listened without eagerness as the scholastic machine worked: every reference to for example prudence, found anywhere in Revelation, was neatly digested into a tidy little dehydrated definition. No one stood up and objected to this, although there were objections enough at other times. Other matters were of greater interest and, besides, the professor didn't seem any more interested in this dead material than were the students.

In the dozen years since, many wonderful things have happened to theology. And, as all the great truths of Christianity fall into clearer focus, we are returned even more firmly to the need to live the Christian life. Which is to say, the life of the virtues. All the grand plans are exciting but sooner or later we

7

have to get down to living them out personally. It was at this particular point—while dealing with CFMers, Newmanites, parishioners and converts—that I began to feel acutely uncomfortable. All these folks, having seen the big picture, were beginning to ask personal questions.

To be personal with us God became a man—not like man, not just clothing his immensity in a human coat for visibility or intelligibility, but really man. Consequently, Christianity is essentially a personal religion. It is as persons devoted to Jesus that we form his People. We are not Christian if we love anything or anyone more than him. It is someone, not something, we receive in communion. It is as personal samples of God's long-suffering love that we, living human men and women, are to be Christ in our world. After all, all Christian history is the product of God's urge to be more personal with us, for love must be personal to be love at all.

Somehow we have succeeded in thwarting God's purpose. We so emphasize the mystery of Jesus that we fail to see how normal he is. Instead, we should get to know him as directly as we can. We should attempt to approach him as normally as his uniqueness will permit. We can learn much by trying to come to know him as we would try to get to know anyone else.

My thesis rises or falls on whether this is what Jesus wants us to do. It is my quiet contention that our Lord sought to communicate and develop the virtues in his apostles and disciples by letting them get to know him. Their daily contact with Jesus, their amazements and misunderstandings, the whole pattern of their rambling three years with Christ—all this, the very experience of living with Jesus, formed them into Christians. We have been long familiar with the way Christ gradually unfolded his saving doctrines. It should not surprise us that he was just as definite in promoting and developing the Christian life.

Friendships, too, have their structure, even though they are gentler and hardly abstract.

So we are going to follow Jesus through the gospel accounts as they have been dovetailed chronologically by Father M. J. Lagrange. This is to rehearse, as much as we can, the very sequence of events lived out by the apostles. The virtues emerge in a fresh and natural sequence, in an order not quite textbookish but friendly. The apostles are to learn them by way of imitation, by way of a shared life with Christ. The Pentecost experience would bring all they had learned to a blazing summary; yet it is essentially an action on the experience they had with Jesus.

Following this path through the gospels I found the virtues become for me warm and personal extensions of my attachment to our Lord. I pray the same may be true for you. This is, experience reminds us, the way we encounter any person, however divine. If it is Jesus we love, him we live for, him in whom we live and move and have our being—most of all, if it is him whom we serve—who else must we yearn to know perfectly? Learn of me, Jesus cries, to every soul that listens.

Lastly, I should indicate that this book has no final summary or conclusion. Over the centuries many have been drawn. Yet each of us must make his own.

Contents

Follow Me: BE HUMAN

1 HUMILITY

Infancy and Hidden Life

WE ALL KNOW WELL HOW THE GOSPEL STORY BEGINS: A CHILD BORN AND BEDDED IN A CATTLE TROUGH; NEW LIFE BEGUN. It is a world dead asleep but for a few shepherds hurrying to a cave to see an infant. Wrapped in the mystery of her son, the mother kneels in awe and love beside the manger. Her husband shifts his feet in masculine confusion before such beauty. Only an angel speaks: "Behold, I bring you good news of a great rejoicing for the whole people. This day, in the city of David, a savior has been born for you, the Lord Christ himself."

We know this scene so well because it is a festival for plain folk, like you and me. The Christmas event, its preludes and its sequels, is shot through with simplicity. Odd as it may sound, for this cast the adjective is ordinary, and normal is the word for its behavior. This is amazing, for what occurs is infinite and unique. God and man become one in a baby named Jesus. Angelic choirs invade our world. Yet, all the same, that birth is wrapped in humility. The airs of the sensational are so removed from its aspect that among all the Christian mysteries we are most at home with Christmas. It is a festival for plain folk.

Or, should I say, for the plain folk you and I wish we were?

Jesus is born into a family that we love at first sight. Every one of us realizes that we are largely the product of our own families. Our attitudes and habits are outgrowths of theirs. For anyone to know us well, they must come to know our forebears. Loving them, then, becomes a reflection of their love for us.

For the little group gathered around the crib, this moment was not so much a beginning as an ending. It was the fulfilment of twenty years of waiting. Each one there thought of the promise Abraham received. This is the special son of David, born in David's town; God has kept faith with his people Israel! It is too easy for us to forget that for Mary and Joseph the Old Testament was not old but still new.

It was their heritage and they were dependent on it. Even God was dependent on it to keep his promise. Mary had not come to the incarnation empty-handed. She brought her humanity and her heritage. She was David's daughter, a Hebrew princess. In her veins ran blood God needed in order that his son be truly Son of Man and Son of David.

Look at Joseph standing there, a great example of religious man. He is just a carpenter, but he knows who he is and to whom he belongs. He does not understand all that has occurred, but he knows that somehow God is visiting his people. He does not demand to know everything; life, he realizes, operates in mystery. Already he has abandoned himself to God's mysterious plans. He has married this virgin; seen her mother a child fathered by God; and heaven only knows what will happen next. Yet so genuinely is this man in a state of peace with God and himself that he can view this scene with complete simplicity.

The shepherds, too, are filled with wonder, yet it was a placid wonder. And as for that absent, and very lovable, family of Zachary and Elizabeth (and their baby John), they were so ordinary that they had been a trifle unprepared when the great angel dived into their lives. Real people, Zachary and Elizabeth, whom we can imagine. We can picture the old man looking over his glasses at Gabriel as he asked if God really could give a child to his old age. His cousin Mary knew better, and didn't ask "can he?" but "how can this be?" Elizabeth later mentioned to Mary how lucky she was in this: "Blessed are you for believing!"—for she was not too pleased with her speechless husband. Despite the realities that surrounded them, the humdrum ups and downs of their long years together, Zachary and Elizabeth did finally open the doors of their home to God's coming. They were a bit hard of hearing, perhaps, but that goes with old age. And they knew, however wonderful their own child was to be, that Mary's child was someone infinitely great. Elizabeth called her mother of the Lord, a title greater even than the full-of-grace the angel named her. What God has joined together—this mother and this child—let no man put asunder.

COMMON TO EVERY ELEMENT OF CHRIST'S COMING IS HUMILITY. God's son arrived into the arms of nobodies, it seemed, born nowhere. Bethlehem and Nazareth could hardly have been dots on any map in Imperial Rome. None of the news media had been alerted to cover the story. Except for the angels who did not restrain their high spirits, everything about the nativity was inconspicuous. And this was the way God wished it to be.

This was to be, and would continue to be for thirty years, because God's son was a man. And our lives—in fact, man's life in general—are inconspicuous. Jesus, being born the right man by virtue of his mother's heritage, must earn his own credentials as a man just as other men earn them, growing up in a home and learning to work.

But, beyond this, God introduces us to his son under these humble circumstances so that we may come to realize the basic necessity of humility in our approach to him. God came to the souls that stood in the straw at Bethlehem because they were humble. Most of all, it is our first glimpse of Jesus himself. And not only this, it will be, first and foremost, as a humble man that he will live out ninety percent of his life. If we are to know Jesus, then, we must ask, what is humility?

OUR AMERICAN ENVIRONMENT TEACHES US THAT NOTORIETY IS THE HANDMAIDEN OF SUCCESS. We learn the necessity of being noticed, of speaking up. We value the concept of independence highly, especially the independence that money brings. Placed in the category "least likely to succeed" are the meek, the humble, the inconspicuous.

We are each taught that, somehow, destiny awaits us, some tremendous act will some day see us recognized, lifted out of the ordinary to "where we belong," among the extraordinary. It is the meek, the Caspar Milquetoasts, we think, who have given up this dream, who are therefore "frustrated," hopeless.

Could it be that we have misunderstood humility as much as our age has misunderstood us?

Humility does not lack boldness. It breeds within us a quiet confidence—a confidence in our secure possession of God and ourselves—that does not frighten and is not fragile before an enemy. With this quiet, confident audacity Mary took exception to the angel's news. Humility does not back down.

Yet it gives us a sense of our limitations. That comes from realizing that we are dependent, that we are just a part in a pattern. Clearly, we are entirely dependent upon God, for he is the good and perfect gift-giver. And it is also obvious to us that the very notion of heredity makes us dependent. We are born into a context, and live within it. Whoever we are when we are being ourselves is so much the product of people other than ourselves! So little of what we admire in ourselves, so few of the attributes others may admire in us, are really ours. Is there even one that we can say was self-produced? These are our real dimensions. We are really dependent, no matter how hard we may try to believe otherwise.

The very heart of a true sense of dependence is reverence. This is an essential characteristic of humility: an awed reverence for the greatness of God, as well as for the greatness he has marked others with, as well as ourselves.

Humility is not just a secret virtue, not simply a private vis-à-vis between God and myself. It is a family virtue, for the family exhibits so clearly our mutual interdependence. The family in Nazareth—Joseph, Mary, and Jesus—were humble, and wrapped every action of their day in the honest mantle of humility.

And their life was full of simple happiness because they appreciated simple joys. Humility lays us open to simple joy. There is within us the capacity for awe, for wonder. If we are humble we can look right at things, all things, and really see them for what they are.

At bottom, humility is the basic orientation of our soul. It is the result of discovering within us the deep presence of God, a presence full of wonder and purpose. Humility is the fruit of learning with our whole mind and heart that God himself is the nucleus of our being; and before we can be anything—or truly be anyone—we must explore this inner space. We must come to know, not just who we are, but whose we are as well.

Our world is peculiarly dead to the absolute magnificence

of God. And we, children of this world, are far from plumbing the immensity of God's grandeur, and the enormity of this further fact: that God lives *in* us. It is he we shall encounter if we explore our inner space. Our independent spirit, our innate self-reliance, comes into the presence of another. We discover then that we are nothing but a receptacle for what gifts God gives. We see that our souls can only escape harm or enslavement in one way or another, by discovering that they belong wholly to God and that they are truly themselves only in the light of his presence, God being their master, and these souls his and his alone.

All this hinges on an awed appreciation of the immensity of God. If this is not real to me, all that I give to this truth is a certain mechanical assent. Then it becomes merely a fact that has been learned—that I belong to God even in the very recesses of my deepest self—and not a truth to live by.

What gives momentum to humility, what makes it live and move, is love. I think humility is falsely termed a passive virtue, as if it were inert. Whether humility shows itself in making little of oneself, preferring quiet or prayer—or even abjection— it is an active virtue. It expresses the decided, urgent preference for loving God, for enjoying his presence before all else. Attending to him becomes what we love most to do.

HERE IS THE KEY TO THE BRILLIANT HUMAN LOVE OF THOSE HIDDEN YEARS IN NAZARETH. Each being truly humble, those three people shared between them their love of God. Its appearances were humbly shrouded in simple events—mother and son carrying jars, talking on their way to the village well; the carpenter and his helper busy in the shop; or all three around their humble table—here was humility mixed with the Infinite.

This is not to say that the infancy and hidden life were

years of perfect peace. Humility must be tested to grow. Tragedy strikes ordinary lives. The family has to flee. They must live in Egypt as displaced persons, as refugees. And how could any mother forget, when she heard of it, the murder of the babies in Bethlehem? Simeon had told her that her soul would be pierced, and this was only the first thrust.

We make the life in Nazareth unreal if we clothe it in untroubled, perfect bliss. These are the fractious townfolk who will later try to kill their neighbor Jesus. Such was their reputation that the whole nation would wonder whether "any good could come out of Nazareth." No, humility does not live in a vacuum. The hidden life was ordinary—which is to say, full of the woes and anxieties of homelife. It takes humility to weather storms calmly, a humility that is strong and lasting.

Humility's insight into our souls must be prolonged, and maintained. We must then begin to live with this deepest self. We can then begin to identify what is not us, what attitudes and habits and misconceptions are to be cast off as false. Gradually we can come to see ourselves, not as others see us, but as God sees us, as we are.

This will set us free to love. I am myself, once I discard this false me, so full of clamor for acclaim. To give myself, to love, I must first be in full possession of myself. I must have my inner liberty and, so composed, be completely open and available. This is a work to be done only with humility.

This inner encounter with God must last. We must gradually get to be "at home" with this self within our selves. This should issue in prayer, conversation however wordless. Externally this would add a new dimension to our prayer with the Eucharist, if we were to attain the attitudes Mary and Joseph had while with the really present Jesus at home. Only from humility can true prayer spring.

THIS THEN IS A SURVEY OF THE VIRTUE THAT OPENS THE WAY FOR
ALL VIRTUES JUST AS TRULY AS THE BIRTH AND GROWTH OF CHRIST
INTRODUCES US TO HIS LIFE. It is an unsensational, inconspicuous,
humble, but irreplaceable start. All lives, spiritual and physical,
begin with childhood.

It is a perduring state, not just a phase. We must not
accept humility as a method, as an anticipation, as a prerequi-
site or preliminary to holiness. It is an act of love, and love lives
in the present, not in the future.

The boy who stood before his anxious mother and calmly
declared: "Couldn't you tell that I would be in the place that
belongs to my Father?" was a self-possessed young man who
knew who he was. The mother who would have to "keep in her
heart the memory of all this" was she who (when just as
young) had cried out that "all generations would call her
blessed." These are the remarkable tones of humility. These are
the great things God can do to the lowly.

AT THE SAME TIME, HUMILITY HAS BRED INTO MARY AND JOSEPH
SUCH A DELIGHT IN THE SIMPLE THINGS THAT THEY WITHOUT QUES-
TION FULFILL WHAT THEY CONSIDER THEIR RELIGIOUS DUTIES. The
child is circumcised, and his mother presents God to God in
the temple. Full grown, Jesus will resemble his mother in this
when he defers to John at the Jordan and is baptized "to fulfill
all due observance."

Do not be discouraged in seeking humility. Living the
Christian life often seems to be forever beginning over again.
It is the nature of perfect humility that we may not realize
when we have reached it, yet if this is our problem, if we are
even close to it, let us rejoice in the quandary. It is much more
likely that we have hardly begun. And as we strive afresh to
seek the simplicity that invites the coming of Christ, we must

never forget that true humility begins with, and never outgrows, the humility of Christmas.

And one of us, a plain girl whose wondrous humility welcomed God's wonders, has sung out:

> My soul extols the Lord;
> and my spirit leaps for joy in God my savior.
> How graciously he looked upon his lowly maid:
> Oh, behold, from this hour onward
> age after age will call me blessed!
> How sublime is what he has done for me—
> The Mighty One, whose name is 'Holy'!
> From age to age he visits those
> who worship Him in reverence.

2 FAITH

Opening of the Public Life

THE PEACEFUL DOMESTIC LIFE OF NAZARETH COULD NOT LAST FOREVER. Watching the child Jesus grow into young manhood and, finally, to full maturity, Mary must have increasingly come to dread the day when such simple joy must end. Like the mother of a missionary off to faraway lands, whose knowledge of her son's vocation cannot quell her sadness at the separation, Mary's apprehension was real and maternal. When the day came, we can imagine the blessed mother, as if to delay her son, mentioning the wedding feast over in Cana. She had promised they would attend. But there was no stopping him. The time had come. He had to be about his Father's business. And, he assured her, he would be at Cana, too.

We miss, I feel, much of Mary's greatness if we imagine she knew just what he was going to do. If we credit the blessed mother with full knowledge of Christ's plans, at the same time we subtract from her any need for faith in him. If she was absolutely sure that he would rise, would not his death have been almost too easy to bear? If she had been his confidante in all the steps of his public life, what room was left for that most fundamental of virtues: faith? To be so blessed among women her faith, too, must have been blessed with trial.

Whenever God acts there is obscurity. This obscurity is not in him, of course, but in us. His mystery so permeates his actions that our reason is baffled. Only a word from him can clarify our wonder. If there were no mystery we would know everything and not need to give him our naked trust. In this there is great profit and great agony. And there is no remedy except to remember that God is infinite and inaccessible. We must be the children we are with God.

So when the day came and Jesus strode down the hills of Nazareth toward the valley of the Jordan, he left behind a mother anxious—and, to a degree, baffled—but sure of him. She had a good many things to ponder in her heart (especially as stories of his doings began to filter back to her), and now he was not there with her to help her faith.

"LOOK, THIS IS THE LAMB OF GOD; THIS IS HE WHO TAKES AWAY THE SINS OF THE WORLD!" How these words of the Baptist must have startled his followers! They must have followed John's outstretched fingers with puzzlement, to see the plain figure of Jesus, the carpenter of Nazareth. Why such a strange title for this workman from the hill country? Two of the disciples were curious enough to approach him and ask where he was living now. And at the simplest of invitations—"Come and see"—they began their adventure.

It is one of the most charming pages in the gospels that recounts the bubbling enthusiasms caused by that first afternoon with Jesus. An excited Andrew brought his brother Simon around to meet his discovery, and Simon discovered, much to his surprise, that he was to have a new name. The news flew about the group of fishermen working that part of the lake that a new leader had been found, a leader who was wonderful to know. Philip was gathered into Christ's net, and he landed Nathanael, and so it went.

What did this first encounter with Christ mean to the future apostles? Did they identify Jesus as their divine savior? Hardly. They were delighted with him; he was their new friend; a friend who was unbelievable because despite his upcountry dress they sensed he was special, a leader with a destiny. All Israel had been searching for such a leader, and *they* had found him!

The apostles never had, like us, habitual faith, faith inbred in us from our mothers' knees. For them Jesus was brand new. For us he is someone whom we have accepted from so early in our lives that our faith often remains unquestioned and, usually, childish. But their enthusiasm was hardly very deep. It was a case of love at first sight; they liked this stranger. Before them yet was the baffling experience of trying to discover just who he really was. It would take over a year and a half of living with him before that answer would be given.

To most of us the whole answer is given immediately, yet we leave our faith little more developed than that of those few fishermen tramping off to a wedding feast with their new friend. With them was a person who bore within him the fullness of the divinity. Being with him, their steps toward faith were, every one of them, steps of progress. Instead, too often our faith is nonchalant. Too little does enthusiasm infect our relationship with Jesus.

Were we to begin to explain to another what our faith is, how would we begin? With a discourse on the Church's unfailing defense of Christ's truths, with explanations of sweet reason? Likely as not. Yet witnessing to our faith does not consist only in answering questions. There is another way of introducing others to God's invisible world: to introduce them to our friend, to Jesus. In other words, we must believe in such a way as to make them wonder whether the invisible realm does not in fact exist, whether Christ is not a living person whom we know. When Philip approached Nathanael and was scorned he didn't say, "Let me explain." He said: "Come and see." He had learned quickly, for his words were a perfect echo of what Jesus said to Andrew and John.

WHEN THEY ARRIVED AT CANA THE FUTURE APOSTLES MET HIS MOTHER. As they joined in the festivities they were hardly aware of the dwindling supply of wine. Likely as not it was the arrival of these unexpected (and thirsty) fishermen who brought the problem to a head. Mary said simply, with tones full of maternal direction, "They have no wine." And to this her son surprisingly replied, "Nay, woman, why do you trouble me with that?"—or (in a preferable translation), "Leave that to me, Mother."

Mary is told firmly by her son that this is not the moment she looks forward to, the moment when she will collaborate with him, for his "hour has not come yet." And it will be long in coming. That "hour" finally comes at Calvary when Jesus next speaks to Mary in the gospels and calls her "Woman," mother of us all. Until then she must bear the burden of separation from him. As he gradually unveils his divinity to an unbelieving world she stands offstage, suffering a mother's most severe strain, for she was apart and could not help him. What faith that took!

Before she departs from the gospels for this while Mary leaves us her only recorded command, one full of faith: "Whatever he tells you, be sure you do it." She had faith in her boy.

The apostles were aware that something extraordinary had occurred and saw confirmation of their hopes: God did mean this man to be his agent, his ambassador. They could be sure of Jesus.

In the weeks to follow their security would be tried. Violence awaited them in Jerusalem. How would they react at the terrifying sight of their gentle friend swinging a whip angrily as he drove bewildered money changers from the temple? How afraid they must have been when the powerful Pharisees called him to task! How amazed they were when Jesus, who had acted as if the temple were his not theirs, faced them down and walked away unscathed! The depths of intensity in Jesus certainly must have unsettled them.

That was just the beginning of it. Again and again Jesus would confound antagonists, dispel devils and, right before their eyes, restore withered limbs and withered hearts! The very spectacle of it bewildered them. A pattern begins to appear. Before doing his wonders he requires faith from the sick and needy. He *demands* faith, confidence in himself. His miracles, it seems, are conditioned upon the vigor of the subject's faith. Sharing the treasures he contains, it is clear, is only possible to the faithful.

Faith consists in placing such credence in another that we believe anything told us. This is the way that we, as children, believed our mothers or fathers. It may be that this experience is still the basis for our faith in Christ. If so, our disposition lacks ingredients of true religious faith. The person whom we completely trust must be God—no one else will do. He who speaks to our faith is God himself, and this, I am sure you will agree, makes a great deal of difference! What we accept, realizing it is God's word, is as true as God is.

Furthermore, what God proposes for our belief—what he

wants us to learn about—is always himself, some secret, some aspect of his own mystery. Never merely factual, all the truths we are to absorb are personal, they are about him, and his Father. Whether a young man paralyzed in his cot or a young woman prostrate in her sin, faith is the key to their recovery. How often the apostles heard Jesus challenge the faith of those who approached. How regularly were they dismissed with the words, "Go in peace, for your faith has saved you!"

From faith all begins. As the apostles struggled with the irrefutable fact that "power went out from him," their faith was just beginning. It is the essential beginning, for it is faith that gives the love Christ means to teach them, and us, both its structure and its development. We cannot expect to love as God would have us love without knowing, through faith, what the mystery of God's own love is. Yes, from faith all begins. Not even true love can exist without a right faith.

Right faith introduces us to new worlds, the very realm in which God lives. Faith brings us news beyond our own creation. God's kingdom, if we be born again, brings us into contact with "what passes in heaven." And all this is as unseen as the wind; it is supernatural. It takes birth "by the breath of the Spirit" to share these ultimate realities, and baptism gives this new life to us only if we believe in him "who has come down from heaven."

This is what Nicodemus heard one night. Over and over again Jesus had but one answer to Nicodemus' amazed query, "How can such things come to be?" Over and over again the Lord repeated, "Believe me, believe me. . . ."

The Christian mystery is always insensible, and must be so. God is spirit, his world and his wisdom are ever supernatural, ever above us. We can only enter that realm through the Word of God, by believing that what Jesus tells us is, simply, the gospel truth. The senses do not help here. They do not see or feel truth. Unmoved and confused, we then come to realize how naked, how unsupported, is the step of faith. It is a naked adhesion to God's word, a word made flesh in Jesus.

This total trust once committed, the final disposition is like that of a confident child. Is this not contradictory? No, now the object of our faith is God; his knowledge is what we share and treasure. Now nothing can alter our stand, for our faith is firm—not because we now understand, but because it is founded in God's truthfulness. This is beyond any confidence a child might possess, and yet it is quite the same, for we are then taking up our positions as God's children, learning from him. Nicodemus, it seems, was too sophisticated for such docility. His confidence in God had grown too stiff and old to learn quickly. Faith that is spontaneous and quick is childlike.

Such spontaneity is a compound of many dispositions. There is mixed in it a thorough awareness of authority, that the Master bears God's credentials. Insight into God's greatness and his care for us is there as well. Humility is at its roots. And, further, there is a note of great need. Perceiving how incomplete we are, how distant we have become from God, when the chance comes to learn of him we are ready to jump at it.

This is the kind of man the centurion was. "Lord, I am not worthy . . . say only the word." He knew what it was to be in the presence of authority. Humility was there. The great need of his servant was agonizing him.

So clear was the centurion's vaulting confidence in Christ that Jesus turned "in amazement" to his followers to say, pointedly, "Believe me, I have not found faith like this, even in Israel!" Such utter loyalty was not yet theirs.

Why not? As we re-read the familiar account of Christ's early ministry perhaps we wonder how the identity of Jesus so long escaped them. In this we do them an injustice. Theirs was a problem man had never faced before. And, further, a problem only God could solve.

This friend of theirs, how were they to make him out? Now they knew his poor beginnings in Nazareth; they had seen his own people try to murder him. He ate, slept and tired like other men. They had seen pity in his eyes before a leper, anger before Pharisees, penetrating love as he looked at each of them. All this was rare enough, but every once in a while the carpenter would master death and demons. Their friend would act with power frighteningly beyond man's strength. Jairus' daughter had felt his touch, the only child at Naim brought back from burial. Countless times had not lame walked, blind seen, and lepers gone off at a run to seek out the priests? Their own nets had been strained with catches beyond their wildest fisherman-dreams. Who could forget, once it had been seen, how Jesus had soothed the wildman of Gerasa and then sent the swine charging, wild as demons, over the cliff?

How, I ask you, were these plain fishermen to make sense of all this? Surely they burned with loyalty to him as he defended them to the Pharisees for breaking the Sabbath, but how had things come to such a pass that they, and their Master, had overturned the Sabbath? They knew they belonged to him, belonged with him, wanting to serve him always, but they were perplexed beyond measure. This man was a mystery to them. "What kind of man is this," they said to one another, "who is obeyed even by the winds and the sea?"

We ought to wonder whether we have lost something in not being as amazed at Christ, as startled by his mystery. The closer we come to Jesus—when suddenly we find him right in front of us—that is when we realize the need for faith. To confront Christ only utter faith will do; anything less means we are not really seeing him, for he is a mystery to us.

He was beyond all marveling. How could they—most of all as fishermen—believe their eyes as Peter strode dry-shod on waves? How could Peter himself comprehend? "What kind of man" was Jesus? Or was he some kind of God? They were beyond their depth, beyond all men's depth. Surely "the flesh is of no avail" here.

"This is what I meant," Jesus told them, "when I said that no one can come to me unless he has received the gift from my Father." Still they could not comprehend. Only that gift would give them some understanding. All about them was confusion at that moment in Capharnaum. All the other disciples, hundreds of their companions for months past, had deserted Jesus. All of them had had "the Lord for their teacher," . . . had listened but had not "learned." When Jesus had finished crying out his great promise to be their very food—"It is my flesh, given for the life of the world"—the apostles, too, felt this was strange talk. But their growing faith was not so little that they would echo the words of the faithless: "This is strange talk, who can be expected to listen to it?" Peter knew he was expected to listen to it, however strange it was, because God spoke through Jesus. And when the Master turned from watching (with such infinite sadness!) the departure of all the rest and courageously asked if the twelve, as well, had heard more than they could bear, the answer was clear and faithful. "Your words, Lord, are the words of eternal life"; where else can we hear God's voice?

After this crisis the gift from the Father was not long in coming. The apostles had been steadfast in their trust; however out of the reach of their comprehension, the value of divine truth is beyond all counting. Steadfastness is the common quality faith engenders; martyrdom is its crown. Faith gives birth to a loyalty to the death, and unflinching possession of this pearl of great price. This quality is to be essential to the apostles' task. To guard and proclaim the good news, the deposit of faith, is exalted among the functions of the Church and guaranteed forever by God. The Church is to become the instrument through whom Christ will, through the centuries, keep his truth true and alive. We cannot separate faith from obedience to the Church's message. They are one and the same.

This was certified forever when Peter's future identity was revealed as the Church's rock-foundation. Yet this can only come after faith. Total faith, only faith leaping to God's conclusions, can permit such collaboration. And there in the solitude of Caesarea Philippi, when Jesus asks his twelve, "Who do you say that I am?" Peter blurts out the identity of their friend. It is the unthinkable, unimaginable solution to the riddle of Jesus: "You are the Son of the living God"; You are God, truly, and truly man. "And Jesus answered him, 'Blessed are you, Simon son of Jona; it is not flesh and blood, it is my Father in heaven that has revealed this to you.'"

God the Father has given the answer no man could guess. Because "the Father had drawn them," had given the divine gift of faith, the apostles could now begin to know him. They know who he is, and this truth overwhelms their souls. For Jesus it is a moment of ringing joy. He is full of gratitude towards Peter and the others, but most especially to his Father, the gift-giver.

Faith is a gift only God can give; it cannot be forced. Jesus had waited through eighteen months for its flowering, for the suitable development of disposition in the twelve that the gift be received freely and fully. Faith is something alive, a living process, surging in a living person, addressing itself to a living God. It is God who does this to us. With a lightning stroke he cuts through the clouds of human wondering. He opens a vista of such clarity that the mind cries out with joy before truth it could not have guessed or dreamed of. Far beyond John Baptist's "joy at hearing the bridegroom's voice," faith exults like a fountain of living water, banishing thirst for all else.

Such is the warmth of this work of the Holy Spirit that the believer knows God through the heart as well as the mind. This is much like the way one who loves me will know intuitively something about me that cannot quite be put in words. This glowing breadth in faith's contact with Jesus makes us continually more and more receptive to his truth, to his word. Only the totality of heaven will give it absolute fulfillment. Until then faith is at the root of our lives.

IT IS NOT FROM OUR LORD THAT WE LEARN WHAT IT IS TO HAVE FAITH. He does not possess it; he is its own object. We see instead the virtue of faith growing up all along his path in all sorts of souls. We see it in stages of development, apprehending in various degrees the depths of truth within Jesus. Where does each of us belong on that scale? Are there signs of growth in our faith, or has it stiffened with age? Or has it never grown beyond infancy?

"Come and see." Our answer is to be found in him, with him. In our most personal encounter with Christ, our soul is open to all the truth that is in him and disposed to all he may teach us. "Whatever he tells you, be sure you do it." This is the whole answer, Mary's answer, to that repeated call of her son to us, "Believe me ... believe me...."

Surrounded today with our complexities, it strikes me as of paramount importance that we be deeply concerned over the quality of our faith. Christian love will, so to speak, take care of itself if our faith is right, for from faith charity gains both its structure and development. In these times faith has not changed but we and our world have. At our worst moments there is a storm that rages around us. Within our hearts we can feel waves of selfishness, doubt and pride. Sometimes the frail hull of our spirit seems about to shatter.

When all at once Jesus speaks to us, as to Peter: "Take courage," he says, "it is myself; do not be afraid."

And we, with Peter, answer, "Lord, if it is yourself, bid us come to you over the water."

The Master's invitation is ever the same: "Come!"

3 PURITY OF HEART

The Sermon on the Mount

SHORTLY AFTER JESUS CHOSE TWELVE FROM AMONG HIS FOL-
LOWERS WHO WOULD BE FOR HIM SPECIAL LIEUTENANTS, HE BEGAN
TO UNFOLD TO THEM THE WHOLE SPIRIT OF HIS NEW KINGDOM.
Now they must seek to form in themselves the spirit of this
new body, an esprit de corps truly Christian.

On a gentle hillock sloping down to Galilee's sea, the
Master began to speak as he had never spoken before. Not only
did he teach, he became a lawgiver who pleaded no precedent,
made no claim to tradition. With precision and gentleness he
unearthed the old law they had always lived by and transformed it into something new. Freeing it from the rubble of
time he lifted it up, opening all its doors and windows to new
air, and placed it on a new foundation as firm and exalted as
himself. He did all this "as one with authority"; not explaining, just declaring it to be so, God's authority alone sufficing.
He had come to "fulfill," "to bring to perfection."

The sermon on the mount does not provide us or the
apostles with a blueprint of the kingdom nor a summary of

Christ's doctrine nor a treatise on Christian morals. Jesus gives us, instead, something far more important. All these other truths will come in their time. First of all, we must catch the spirit of his kingdom. In all its freshness and beauty we must, before all else, see the vision of happiness he offers and its cost. In the sermon on the mount Jesus would give aspirants to his kingdom a clear definition of its goal of perfection, its new spirit.

Seated there on the hillside, he begins by pointing to its mountaintops, the beatitudes. Happy is the man ("blessed are you") if these mountaintops oversee our life, if our love scales these heights. One by one he extols the happiness he will provide to satisfy the hunger in every man. Eight happinesses are named, eight amazing ways to revolutionize our worldly idea of joy. In reality, though, they are all the same happiness, a happiness obtained in eight ways, a happiness one and several since it comes from a single source, God's one spirit of joy.

The beatitudes reveal their secret unity when we realize that we are only happy when we are like Jesus. Although he is himself their exemplar, Jesus does not point to this pattern. The Master does not speak of himself at all until the eighth beatitude, and then he only intimates that he himself explains them all. The apostles are not ready to understand that the Master will be persecuted, a target for malicious lies, and all because he lives this life of perfect beatitude. Even the revelation that he is "meek and humble of heart" is saved until later. Yet it must have been transparent that he was speaking of what he knew within himself.

And what do the beatitudes say? They proclaim that man is given the happiness of hungering and thirsting to be like God. The great freedom of heart God shows is offered to us if we can form within ourselves the soul of a poor man. The poor enter the kingdom on the ground floor. Their condition prepares them for it—nothing they have is in the way of their trusting entirely in God. He can be their whole life; a man has to be really poor to look to our Father for everything. Prizing God as their only treasure, everything else they possess can be so easily given away. If we are poor in fact or in spirit the effect is freedom: we are unburdened of all the luggage of possessions to leap after him. "Blessed are the poor in spirit; the kingdom of heaven is theirs."

This is not to be thought of unrealistically, Jesus quickly adds: "Blessed are those who mourn; they shall be comforted." Mourning is to be expected; it will be thoroughly discouraging to be treated like a nobody. Being poor will be difficult. It will invite external affliction. The temptation will arise to go back and cling to something that will affirm our identity before others, something that will show we have ability or knowledge. To this Jesus replies with assurance of deeper happiness, comfort from him now and in eternity. What deeper comfort exists than the knowledge that, whatever the tribulation, it will be like his—the comfort, then, of knowing we are like Jesus. Our deepest identity is securely marked with his; our resignation bears his reward.

This leads us into the quiet plains of meekness. Patience and inner poise come of "possessing the land" surely, of having the kingdom of God both within us and before us. From meekness flows true assurance, true confidence that no violence can hurt us, that God will order all things well. Exercising courage, never being afraid of anything, makes us firm and strong, and only the strong can be meek. We gravely mistake true meekness if we make it equal being insipid or craven. Instead, it leads us to know that we do not have to be "pushy," that we do not need to spread anxiety on others or ourselves. It can endow us instead with the startling composure that overcomes, without a blow being struck, any obstacle to God's will. This security marks every step of Christ's life. If we can release ourselves fully into his hands, such happiness will be ours: "Blessed are the patient; they shall inherit the land."

"Blessed are those who hunger and thirst after holiness; they shall have their fill." If our inner anxiety seeks any outlet let it be in thirsting after holiness, justice before God. There is a dead justice and a living justice; and justice dies from the moment it becomes a comfort—when it ceases to be a burning reality, a demand upon oneself. Such a quest brings with it satisfaction and completion if its goal is high enough. To do so with an urgency—hungering and thirsting—will not only bring full satisfaction at life's end, Jesus promises, but inner joy and relief all along the way to his Father, for so it is with himself. Only those know this who have tried to become utterly what God wants them to be; this Jesus knows. It is a harrowing experience to measure our own souls by God's yardstick. This could produce in us fear and anxiety that would lead us to desperation. Yet at the same time God always gives us hope that, if we let him, he can make even us holy. Once we know this there is nothing else to hunger and thirst for: it is the only true happiness.

Mercy is a divine attribute. The greatest glory we can give to God is to be saved by him. It is the most perfect happiness we can provide him. Saved from ourselves, purified by his holiness, this can only be his work. For any man who knows how greatly he needs God's mercy on himself there is only one course to take, and that is to be merciful to everyone else. The happiness Jesus promises to the merciful is no different from what his own is. It is not the sure gratitude of those who experience mercy—that often does not come. It is, rather, the further untroubled happiness of being like God, whatever the reaction. "Blessed are the merciful; they shall obtain mercy." Any other reward is cheap and temporary by comparison, as is any other happiness.

The same is true of peace-making. So many have spent their whole lives exhausting themselves to make peace. It made them like God, his children, like God's son. Little matter if all their efforts did not bring full peace to earth; it is enough that they were like God. They were samples of him on earth. Anyone seeking to create God's peace on earth is not promised the happiness of seeing it come to pass; the promise is more divine than that. "Blessed are the peace-makers; they shall be counted the children of God." Simply by being here they will have had the happiness of exemplifying God.

The key to this is held in the last beatitude. This life is necessarily full of persecution for conscience' sake. It is by design a time of trial and inequity. We know our struggles for perfection will always involve agony. But this is not a happiness, and this is not what Jesus speaks of. It is persecution for his sake that beatifies. That we would suffer for our inadequacy, that our faults would lead us into collision with our world and ourselves is not surprising. In this we are hardly persecuted, because we do deserve these humiliations. But to be truly happy is to be so like Jesus that we are treated like him, that we are persecuted because he was. "Blessed are those who suffer persecution in the cause of right; the kingdom of heaven is theirs." This is the last beatitude because it is so high. All the other seven go to make up the man so like Jesus that he would clearly be persecuted, as Jesus said, "because of me." What happiness there is in knowing we are so like him, so full of him, that we are mistaken for him.

THESE ARE CLEARLY THE MOUNTAINTOPS OF THE CHRISTIAN LIFE, THE LIFE OF THE SPIRIT. But Jesus did not expect full understanding of such immense truths as quickly as the apostles heard these eight sentences. The rest of the sermon on the mount did not even elaborate them completely. Yet once and for all the goal was set: we were invited to become what we all want to be—but which seems utterly impossible—to be like God. "You are to be perfect," the Master will repeat a few minutes later, "as your heavenly Father is perfect."

What was most essential was that the apostles begin to seek perfection. And what struck them most deeply about this vision, this new spirit? Which beatitude would most immediately strike their hearts? I feel it was the one we have not yet discussed: "Blessed are the clean of heart, for they shall see God."

It is a tremendously graphic idea: to have our hearts clean, pure of all stain, unobstructed, spontaneously clear. It is the very negation of all the duplicity and hypocrisy that smears our world. It is expressive of total openness. The clean, open heart is open to all hearts, all open to the love in Jesus' heart. It possesses a pure honesty that no one could challenge. There is none of the murky confusion of motives that clouds our acts and thoughts. This need not be a heart never tarnished, like Mary's, but one that, in whatever way, is finally like the heart of Jesus. It is frequently a heart that feels its senses seeking to confuse and rebel. It is, ultimately, your heart and mine as God wants them to be, and as we profoundly would have them be, for that would be the greatest of happiness. It would mean our hearts would be like God's, and that we surely could see him for all eternity—and even now within ourselves.

This purity of heart is the first order of business for the apostles. It is to become the striking characteristic of the new kingdom. It is founded on humility and faith. Only with the special supernatural humility and faith that Jesus has already taught them can the disciples so open their hearts for his cleansing. Putting aside all else, it is with a singlehearted devotion that they must follow him, with hearts becoming as single-hearted as his own. Nothing else must cloud their hearts; for them no riches must exist but himself. As Jesus points out, "Where your treasure-house is, there too your heart is bound to be."

Humility and faith collaborate in clarifying our hearts; it is the effect, in part, of what has gone before. Yet no amount of hungering and thirsting on our part can bring it about. God gives us this purity; only he can bring our efforts to this perfection. Finally we become fully exposed to his influence, open to all he wants us to do and to be. What this means is that this clarity is not given to us for our own enjoyment, as something personal and private. It is given for his purposes; it is a public gift.

"You are the salt of the earth . . . the light of the world." Through you, Jesus tells us, I mean to light this world that is so dark, I mean to make it taste my happiness. Through you this can come to be if you do not obstruct my grace, if your hearts are clean. So much depends on this, that you let me clearly transmit my image through you to the world.

To fail in this is to be as insipid as spent salt. If the world, as it passes, spurns the disciple who loses his fervor, it is Jesus who is spurned. If our hearts are refracted and impure, God's light is blocked and as useless as a light under a basket. The dark is not enlightened; the light cannot pass. Such is the social importance of purity of heart. God needs the pure of heart to get into our world, to show himself to us.

This requires from the apostles a sanctity and a spirit higher than that of the Old Testament. What the new spirit does to the old order is not to set it aside but to complete it. Jesus gives five different examples of how the old law is amplified by the new. The essential point of each is that now the moral life we lead must be total. Externals are no longer enough. What proceeds from a pure heart exhibits and demands inner goodness, total goodness. Whole, entire dedication is needed. A man can foul himself in his heart, out of sight of all human detection. And Jesus wants us to give ourselves to him completely, to become totally suffused by this new spirit.

All this is because he invites his followers to a new level of union with him. He is preparing us to be his friends. He is inviting us to share in God's family spirit: its purity, its warmth, its perfection. Like himself and like his Father, he would have us give in to one another, and help one another without stint— each yielding where our rights are concerned, not insisting on them. This is to let our brother, who may be wrong or unfair, have his way, so that we might correct him by our gentleness and so keep peace in the family. Justice, strict justice, was the theme of what "was said to men of old"; now familial love is to dominate. Now we are to "turn the other cheek," to go the extra mile.

This is to become samples of God, his reflections. Not to reply to violence in kind is to witness to the one who makes "his rain to fall on the just and equally on the unjust." Love an enemy, an intruder, a stranger—then, Jesus promises, "your reward will be a rich one, and you will be *true sons* of the most High, generous like him towards the thankless and unjust. You see," the Master concludes, "you are to be perfect, as your heavenly Father is perfect." We are to give and forgive like him. This is the new spirit. This calls for absolute purity of heart.

WHEN DID EACH OF US FIRST HEAR THE BEATITUDES? Probably it was as children that we first put to memory this outline of the true Christian spirit. And every time they are quoted, what is our reaction? Is it sentimental? Wishful? Do we look through the sugarcoating our emotions may have baked over them to see them realistically? Honestly, our natural reaction to the sermon on the mount ought to be one of distaste. Wouldn't we naturally think that the happiness would include wealth, pleasure, and worldly peace? What Jesus has done is to contradict directly our worldly concept of happiness. Far better that we face it than unthinkingly accept the sermon and the beatitudes as pious platitudes. What the apostles heard was not a placid dissertation on virtue; it was a declaration of independence, a declaration of war.

It is a beautiful vision Jesus unveils of how wonderful human life might be. But is it possible? Can man be so good? Our commonsense tells us no, that this is idealism run rampant. And this is true except for the crucial fact that it is God who invites us, and will enable us to live this new life of the spirit. The beatitudes, for man's strength alone, are unreachable, untenable paradoxes. God makes them livable, for it is to a life like his that we are called. No longer just his creatures, we are to be his friends, his sons.

The Master does not want anyone of us to enter his kingdom unless we realize the cost. No reward is sure until the end; no motive is offered but ultimate, eternal happiness with him. In between now and then, struggle and weakness are to be expected. So, lest we misunderstand, Jesus points to two cures for sentimentality, two harsh descriptions of the new spirit's difficulty.

The first refers to the achievement of purity of heart. We must impose on our complexity God's simplicity, which requires a real surrender of self. We must learn to give as God gives, not looking for the world's reward. Our prayer is to be the prayer of a sinner who looks neither to the left or right. To yearn for the world's approval is to undercut any real denial in our self-denial. We give nothing to God that way, for we take nothing from ourselves. This makes our souls mirrors reflecting ourselves and no more. We must not see ourselves; we must forget ourselves; we must not "let our left hand know what our right is doing."

This is to be detached. Almsgiving helps us to unload the luggage of the possessions we weigh ourselves down with, and bravely to call it all excess baggage. Prayer affirms this dedication to God when we separate it from all other approval and stay just with him. Fasting cuts deeper to the bone to try and set up a new order in ourselves, a new spirit wherein we are his disciplined servants. If a man is to give himself he must first possess himself. Not to strike back, to see our egoism and pride undone, to give to our attacker—these are not works of sentiment. They take discipline, dedication, purity of heart. We cannot love like Christ until we reach this degree of inner poverty and humility.

On the other hand, the second task checks another source of self-satisfaction. "Judge nobody," Jesus warns. Taking all men as our friends means judgment is out of place, for a friend does not sit in judgment. We must give our tolerance, our indulgence to everyone but ourself. Look for the spot in our own heart first of all, and we will discover we will have job enough removing just it. Our meekness is for others, our criticism for ourself. To judge is to feel superior, and in our condition of inner disorder, to be hypocritical.

The counterfoil for all of our Lord's teaching here is those Pharisees who opposed him. They are the externalists; they sit in judgment. They stand self-indicted of hypocrisy. The values they proclaim contract the beatitudes. They fail to seek happiness beyond the immediate. It can all be summed up by saying that their hearts were not open but closed, unclean, impenetrable. This is why Jesus could not do the obvious thing and take his message and his credentials to the high priest and Pharisees for their approbation. It was not to the "wise and prudent" he could come. The self-secure would not face such a disturbing, agonizing re-evalution. The poor in spirit, the clean of heart are his listeners, open, unfettered, honest enough to admit their need.

It is easy enough to picture the hypocrisy of these Pharisees. Yet clear as their image is, we must not forget that it is painted for our profit. Courageously we must wonder whether we, too, are such Pharisees. Do not point the finger elsewhere; point it at ourselves. The really frightening thing about the Pharisees is that they are so human, so imaginable. And, it needs to be said, unhappy. Should we feel superior to them? By what right? If we have grounds, it is by God's grace and nothing in us. We can have prejudice towards no one. Only God can, and such is his love for all of us that he chooses not to prejudge anyone. Our first business is with ourselves.

Jesus closes the sermon on the mount with solemn assurance that this new spirit he presents is essential. No happiness lasts that is found elsewhere. No other treasure-house will stand. No other leader will know the way. He is our guide and our support. And lipservice to his ideals will not suffice; only the man who "does the will of the Father," who "hungers and thirsts after holiness," will gain entrance to the kingdom. Crying "Master, Master" is not enough unless we put our heart into it.

THE NEW SPIRIT, THE CHRISTIAN SPIRIT, IS THE SPIRIT OF JESUS. He wants to give this to us, to give himself to us. But this is not possible unless we meet its terms and form a fit home for it. The Christian spirit is not partial or slight; we must let it penetrate us entirely. We must expose ourselves, uncovering all our secret corners of hypocrisy and self-love. Jesus wants to permeate us like oil in a fabric. And how we must yearn for this goal, for he has told us of its happiness.

Beyond the figure of Mary, his mother—whose beauty is based on the clarity of her virginal heart—there emerges (shortly after this day on the hillside) another Mary not unlike the first. Would it be rash to suppose that the Magdalen was among Christ's hearers on the mount? Present or absent, she had learned by heart the lesson proclaimed. No self-consciousness shows as Mary Magdalen washes the Master's feet and dries them with her hair. She brings us our first glimpse of fullhearted response to Jesus, and it is not surprising that it is a woman's love that first breaks through. Notice its purity, the sense of honor in it. There is nothing of the possessive in her devotion to Jesus. There is in this sinful woman made clean none of the superiority the Pharisee pretends. Whatever her history, it is gone now; her heart has leaped to beatitude.

Which brings us to the point that underlies, and completes, our whole subject here. Purity of heart, a heart open and exposed, is the condition to true friendship; so much so that friendship is limited to the degree that such purity pre-exists. It is the matrix of friendship, its common ground. God's friendship is, wonderfully, ours for the asking if we ask with all our heart. Yet we must try to match God's friendship for us. This clean heart in us allows God to treat us as his friend. Heart speaks to heart in friendship. No rights, no justice, intervene. The new spirit is a spirit of friendship, incredible friendship with God and all that is his.

Imagine its effects. Friendship either presupposes equality, or brings it about. There is never even a suggestion of condescension. This is important for it influences what follows friendship with Jesus. To everyone else we must be friend in his name. What is expected of us today may well be a renewal, a rebirth of the friendship which ought to exist throughout the world. How absent it is! And from what other source can it come than purity of heart? Anything of the contrived or artificial just deepens suspicion. We must dare to be true friends to everyone in a world that no longer knows what it is to befriend. This is to bear the new spirit of Christ; all men will then know us as his disciples.

This is the perfection to which we are invited as hearers of the Master's sermon on the mount. He has shared with us the secrets of happiness, and the heights to which we are called. Now that we have seen these mountaintops, and know the road, let us set out one step after another—even one leap after another. The going gets easier as we leave more and more of the luggage of self behind, for Jesus himself assures us that happy "are the clean of heart, for they shall see God!"

To catch the unique spirit of Jesus, nothing must keep us from learning this by heart.

4 PRUDENCE

The Kingdom Parables:
Messianic Crisis

IT WAS A FULL NINE MONTHS AFTER THAT DAY ON THE MOUNTAIN-
SIDE BEFORE JESUS DIRECTLY WARNED HIS TWELVE THAT THEY
"MUST BE WARY AS SERPENTS, AND YET INNOCENT AS DOVES."
Christian simplicity does not wander carelessly through a world
it contradicts. In no way does purity of heart absolve the
Master or his followers from realism. There is, indeed, no true
virtue without prudence, for being "simple" has some overtones
that do not fit the Christian description.

In the months that preceded this summary statement Jesus
gave the apostles a great object lesson in prudence. It began
immediately after his relatives made an attempt to restrain him.
Suddenly the frank, direct teaching of the Master is veiled. He
speaks now in riddles that baffle the chosen band, so long
accustomed to letting their Lord do their thinking for them.
Their minds do not want to try to unravel parables. Why does
Jesus do this to them?

As soon as they can get him alone it is the first question

they ask: Why, Lord? And he simply replies: "Because it is granted to you to understand the secrets of God's kingdom, but not to these others." For the first time in the gospels something covert, something of the devious, is introduced. Still, Jesus is being openly mysterious; the challenge to listen and learn is extended to all "that have ears to hear with."

There are great clouds forming that dictate this change in technique. Could the Pharisees ignore the harsh indictments this new teacher has hurled at them? Could they let pass Christ's claim to legislate a newer law than theirs? By now their counter-attack is planned; among the ears hearing Jesus are ears intent now only on his downfall. Now is a time for Jesus to be wary. He is not upset by this surveillance. Undaunted, he will confound the wise. But yet another obstacle looms: the popular mind. His listeners are beginning to hear only what they want to hear. The radical news of his kingdom is muffled by centuries of misunderstanding. Not of this world, the new kingdom has its life and its triumphs within the secrecy of hearts, not in the grandiose, material arena of wealth or politics. Indeed he is the Christ, the Messiah, but not the one they expect.

Jesus has detected this great danger of misunderstanding on the part of the crowd. Their idea of the messianic kingdom— a national kingdom with another David on Sion's throne—was as faulty and as fluctuating as their own thoughts and dreams. Through this web of delusion the new truth must seep into their thoughts. The Master proposes parables to dulled hearts, then, to ears slow to listen. Slowly unwound in minds truly searching for truth, the new truth is uncovered within; the hard coatings of the old are dissolved. To them that love only the old, nothing is given. Their ears hear just charming tales without meaning.

Slowed by these factors, Jesus tells the secrets of his kingdom's life in parables. His purpose will brook no delay. In a way adjusted to the circumstances, he teaches those he can reach.

He has so much to tell his apostles. They, too, are slow; explanation after explanation is necessary. Perhaps we are so long accustomed to what the parables mean that we have difficulty in imagining what riddles they were to the twelve. Yet they, above all, must understand them. They are to become this kingdom; to them will fall the task of teaching these truths to the world.

The parables mark, therefore, a sharp change in method by which the Master seeks to unfold his good news. While an enemy forms in pursuit, he must wait for their understanding. It is a problem in prudence that Jesus solves with stories that have charmed all who have heard them with their beauty and economy. All the same, they were not told for their beauty. They were ingenious—not ingenuous—marvels of adjustment, on Christ's part, to a changed climate.

Prudence is the science of adapting our strength to the task before us. If we act prudently we make best use of the power God gives us. The Christian spirit does not live and act in a vacuum; it is surrounded by the myriad factors that others about us introduce. These cannot be ignored, for all of these others are of concern to us. The function of prudence is to assure effective realization of our goals in the flux of the temporal. It seeks to make the real ideal—successfully—to greatest possible effect. Prudence must color every Christian act. It puts the Christian spirit into practice.

What distinguishes true prudence from cold calculation and worldly caginess? Is this not like bare manipulation of the crassest sort? Hardly. Worldly prudence is not suffused with the compassion Christ feels for his slow-witted disciples. He seeks to give eternal truth. All the arch strategies of our world have shorter, selfish goals. He is a teacher seeking the most effective means to teach.

And what does he teach? Each parable begins with the same preface: "The kingdom of heaven is like . . ." In many respects, the kingdom of God is intrinsically *like* the processes of nature and the daily life of men. The remarkable realism and vividness of the parables, their faithfulness to nature, the fact that they are not farfetched and artificial analogies, is due to the affinity which does in truth exist between the natural order and the spiritual order. The kingdom of heaven *is* like a growing crop. The seed is full of a divine fecundity; it will grow of itself, granting good conditions in the soil. Its growth will be as unobtrusive as the miracles of the soil, and those who promote it must be as patient as farmers. Again, the kingdom of heaven *is* like a crop oversown by weeds. Reaping-time is separation time; the harvester waits. In this world of ours the kingdom cannot be a model-farm—such perfection is unrealistic now; it comes later. Toleration becomes us now until judgment intervenes. But there will be no stopping the growth of the kingdom, however insignificant its beginnings. That is why the kingdom *is* like a mustard seed that grows into a tree that welcomes all sorts of birds to its branches. But this will not happen in a flash. It is an inner growth. The grace-laden gospel will, secretly and steadily, permeate the world like leaven does dough. The kingdom does have a leaven all its own. It *is* like a net thrown into the sea—heaven knows it has caught fish of all kinds, bad ones and good ones. It is not for us to try to choose one from the other; we can leave that awesome task to God and his angels.

It is part of prudence to know just what we are about. If

we are to be citizens of this kingdom its laws, which are caught in the simple devices of these parables, must be clearly in our minds. They will give us firm principles, sure-sightedness and circumspection as we gain experience in living in the kingdom. To do without these aids would lead us to many of the impatient excesses of imprudence. We would be forgetting that the kingdom of heaven *is* like the world we live in. It is indeed an organized kingdom. But, however divine, it is one still encompassed by difficulty and sin.

Prudence governs how we proceed. But where are we going? Of what value is the prize we seek? Ah, says Jesus, it is worth all you have and more. The kingdom is the pearl of great price, the treasure full of joy surpassing everything else. Its quest must be in proportion. You must spend everything in seeking it; there will be no waste, for its value is beyond anything else you can possess. Full knowledge of this can bring us great discernment of soul. Knowing deeply what we value above all else, it is so much easier to put proper value on everything else. The path of prudence is cleared; the goal is set. Prudence then becomes love discerning wisely the things that are favorable to our quest and those that are not.

Even though the path is clear and the goal brilliant in our sight, problems remain. It is really difficult—however easy in the abstract—to spend all that we have, to sell everything that is ours. Jesus has stated the quest for us honestly, for it will cost us. It is more than worth all we spend; but however little it is that we have, it is all we have. Detachment is the hard parting that such farsighted prudence must promote. Christian prudence, Jesus tirelessly points out at every opportunity, involves poverty always. In this world of things, poverty and prudence are inseparable, in varying degrees. The prudence of this world leans heavily on riches. Our prudence, Jesus reiterates incessantly, is beyond that because our goal is a heavenly kingdom.

ANOTHER POINT EMERGES FROM THE PERIOD OF THE PARABLES. Jesus is obviously concentrating upon the apostles now, upon the formation of an elite, a band of followers to continue his work and proclaim his message after he is gone. It is not his intention to fulfill his mission single-handed; there must be a company to whom he can entrust it; these must learn even if no one else does. They are going to tend the growing mustard seed; they are going to knead his leaven into the world. The special preparation that our Lord gives the twelve is prudent. Prudence has foresight for one of its marks.

Beginning with Christ's selection of a band of followers, we can follow his graduated efforts to prepare them prudently for the tasks they have yet to comprehend. With them above all, Jesus exhibits the farmer's care, the fisherman's patience. He will not overcome their freedom; their growth will be gently and persistently encouraged. His greatest skill as a master teacher is spent on them, and slowly but surely they respond. Many months were yet to pass, even, before their faith would be clear. But such accomplishments do not happen overnight; they are the work of prudent foresight. What should be a great lesson to us is this sight of Jesus himself so prudently preparing harvesters for a harvest not in sight. And this is done with a restraint that respects their ignorance and their liberty. To achieve this one must start early; it is only prudent. To be true to those closing words of his in the sermons, Jesus must see to it that his house, once he builds it, is dug deep and founded, finally, on rock.

What a teacher! Drawing deep on his human reflections on nature, he explains and teaches huge truths with incredible simplicity. For his true listeners there is flavor and clarity; for the deaf of heart, silence. Much of his mastery is reserved for the twelve. As far as we know, no one else saw him walk on water or watched, with shocked amazement, as his raised hand calmed storms. He was the Lord, but, however immense his power, just as much a master in its use. It can be said that this is just as important as having it. And here again we find ourselves face to face with the virtue of prudence, for it relates precisely to how we use our strength. It has the responsibility of assuring good, supernatural government of oneself and one's resources.

It is always timely, for its every operation is to take place in one of time's moments. History has its numberlessly various ways of happening; every event belongs to just one moment. Consequently, prudence has no stock solutions. The wildman of Gerasa happened at one moment. Suddenly there he was rushing to molest Jesus; at the next moment thrown at his feet. Once this human storm is calmed, Jesus does not ask him to follow along; prudence dictated otherwise. It will not be so with the poor young rich man he meets later. The point is that they are different moments. Every moment requires its own special insight. Yet prudence has this stability: even though there are never two identical situations, prudence constantly and consistently must declare what is the best path towards its final goal. Yet the terrain is ever changing. Prudence always has new problems, and retains its momentary character. Just as we can never touch a river twice in the same place, so time flows by ever various. To bring our morality down to practice, to realistic application in each moment's need: this is prudence's task in an always different world.

A hemorrhaging woman throws caution to the wind and dives at Jesus from behind just to touch the edge of his cloak.

It was clearly the prudent thing for her to do! A persistent Syro-phoenician lady talks back to Jesus—and very prudently—because he is testing the depth of her faith and the extent of her need. The daughter of Jairus dies just at the wrong moment, it seems, for it is in the midst of all the surveillance Jesus is subject to. He does not throw caution to the winds. No one can come with him but Peter, James and John. All the derision and affront of the crowd is prudently borne in order to keep the girl's resurrection as quiet as possible. It was not so at Naim half a year before, when the widow got back her son. Prudence, indeed, has its moments and they are hardly predictable. It is a question of doing, with foresight and insight, the right thing at the moment that is right before us.

All the same, just as prudence has its flexible moments so also it can be inflexible. It is never weak. It can allow no compromise with principle, no deviation that does not clearly lead towards its goal. Witness the scene in Nazareth as the native son comes to visit after his exploits throughout Galilee. A ferment of discontent builds as Jesus does not soften his call to a new spirit with miracles they could boast about. But these are not hearts open to him; it remains true that incredulity incapacitates miracles. A few wonders performed and Jesus could have been Nazareth's hero. One might be tempted to say it would have been prudent to go along with them on this. Danger of death was involved. But prudence does not back down—not true prudence, not Christian prudence—once principle is at stake.

The decision that prudence must reach shortly afterwards in Capharnaum is just as clear-cut. The Lord has fed the multitudes with bread and it has only succeeded, it seems, in feeding their false messianic desires. Again there is a shallow, national mood capable of the spontaneous-combustion Nazareth pro-

duced. So glutted do they become with their own desires that
his words on the true bread from heaven are hardly attended
to. Then he extends the magnificent invitation to become one
with him by eating this bread of life which is himself. They are
shocked. Without faith as a foundation, their sand-castles collapse. And yet with just a word, a "prudent" word of the
worldly sort, Jesus would not have had to watch the crowds
walk off shaking their heads at such "strange talk." What a
travesty of true prudence if Jesus had backed down from the
literal truth he had proclaimed. Prudence does seek to accom-
modate, but it has its very definite limits.

The kingdom the crowds wish is not his kingdom, but a
false one. They are victims of a rigidly preconceived idea; he
will be no earthly king. The purpose of the parables appears in
bold relief. So often the remark has been too quickly made, "I
know just what you mean!" Jesus not only has hammered away
at their misconception, he has tried to penetrate their understanding with the gentle oil of the parables. But they will not
bend. They are going to be really dangerous when they see,
finally, that he will not give them what they want. But prudence has dictated this moment for a test of faith. Prudence
has its own patience, yet it too has its limits.

Soon he sends the apostles off to preach on a practice mission. At the end of his instructions, he enunciates his summary
statement on the need for prudence. "Remember, I am sending
you out to be like sheep among wolves." It is no lark they set
out on; there will be opposition of which they must beware.
Indeed, the Master concludes, "You must be wary, then, as serpents, and yet innocent as doves." Be sure to wear the moral
armor of innocence—it disarms objection by removing anything
which can be attacked fairly. This is truly part of prudence.
But we must go further; we must possess the quickness serpents

have to perceive attack, and elude it. The peace the apostolic visitors will offer on their journey through the towns of Galilee will often be repulsed. After all, could the apostles expect treatment any different from that of their Lord?

Prudence involves experience and deliberation. We expect it to be cautious and circumspect. Unfortunately, in many minds these excellent qualities unite to produce an image of prudence that is quite dull. Haste and negligence surely are defects to be feared, but on no account is all spontaneity out of order for the prudent Christian. Prudence must never be conceived of as the "lay low" virtue, the timid virtue, the virtue that never takes a risk and fears "getting involved." This is to take an entirely negative attitude towards prudence. It makes it into the virtue by which we keep everything safe. Instead, it is the virtue of initiative and responsibility, one that is daring.

What could have been more audacious than the cutting accusations Jesus hurls at the Pharisees who indict the disciples of ritual uncleanness? No peacemaker here, he lashes out at the hypocrisy that underlies this pharisaical judgment. In a moment the whole Old Testament concept of external purity is overthrown. The kosher laws are repealed. The prudent Christ has scandalized the Pharisees. This was really daring and, at the same time, marvelously prudent. In what more vigorous way could the Master have brought to sight his new spirit? Holiness is of the heart, not the hands alone. To put this across he, prudently, chooses to shock; persuasion was not enough. Prudence can be suave but it surely can also legitimately be scandalous.

The prudent, continuous effort of the Master to prepare leaders for his kingdom is bearing fruit. The loyalty of the twelve must have swelled in their breasts as Jesus defended them before the Scribes and Pharisees. When the long wait for the Father's gift of faith finally ended, and the twelve professed their true recognition of Jesus as the God-Man, it is prudence's triumph as well. The Lord has faithfully respected the personal freedom of his band. He has not rushed what cannot be forced.

Peter, then, identifies Jesus; Jesus, in turn, can now identify Peter as the rock. Peter is to be the key figure among the twelve; he will bring solidity and cohesion to the kingdom that the Lord builds. Peter's faith releases from Jesus this blueprint for his Church. It is to be a Church that can weather the ages and the devil's efforts; it is prudently founded on a rock that remains visible in this world long after the founder leaves. Over and over again Jesus has told us that his kingdom *is* like our world— in the basic organization of its authority he has not forgotten this. He has prudently arranged to leave to his Church all the powers it will need.

This, however, does not finish the matter. Prudence is sleepless. It must overlay, not only every action of its great exemplar, the Lord, but every action of the Church and each Christian throughout the rest of time. The only prudent thing to do is to be ever at the task of "following me," Jesus sternly reminds his disciples. It will take harsh self-renunciation; it will mean daily taking up our crosses. It will involve us in the folly and "imprudence" of the Cross. The prudence of Christ is far beyond the wisdom of the world.

For us it does not consist in believing in Jesus or being his friend; Christian prudence commands us to act like him in all the various moments of our lives. For us, nothing else will do; unless we are doing his work nothing has value. All we attempt must be done with sacred care, so high are the stakes at issue. Two questions are all Jesus needed to engrave this need on the hearts of his twelve—and of all the millions who were to come after them after him.

"How is a man the better for it," he asks us, "if he gains the whole world at the expense of losing his own soul?

"For a man's soul, what price can be high enough?"

To these questions the only answer is the prudent answer. And Jesus has shown us what prudence is.

5 PRAYER

The Transfiguration

ONE OF THE MOST STRIKING CHANGES THAT JESUS BRINGS ABOUT BY HIS LIFE AMONG US CONCERNS HIS FATHER. The great God— God the creator of heaven and earth, God the Father—suddenly becomes our Father, someone closer to us than any other father. The God whose greatness, like lightning crackling through the clouds, was untouchable and fearsome, because of Jesus becomes for us an intimate, friendly, approachable, loving Father.

Jesus introduces us into the family of God. We are invited to membership in his kingdom, and it is no ordinary kingdom. Its citizens are to share in the incredible unity God has within himself. In this holy communion the citizen is to be so fused with his king that, as the Master put it, he "lives continually in me, and I in him. As I live because of the Father, the living Father who has sent me, so he who eats me will live, in his turn, because of me!"

It remains a kingdom of faith here on earth. Its very air is breathed only by the faithful; no other eyes can see its landmarks; no other instinct but that of faith can sense its new intimacy. And, like faith, the kingdom is the gift of the Father.

So it is that life with the Father is constantly on Jesus' mind. He is continually at pains to communicate this to us; for him it is the expression of his own inner one-ness. To learn of him as he really is we must seek to penetrate into the inmost life of the God-Man and to hear the most personal whisperings of his heart. Yet little comes to our weak ears, for these whisperings are pitched way up on the plane of the infinite; they are the words that pass between Jesus and his Father, between God and his divine son.

There is one recurrent rubric that dots the pages of the gospels with this mystery. It usually reads, . . . and Jesus "went up by himself on to the hillside to pray." It always occurs before any major new step in Christ's work—how many other times Jesus sought this solitary conversation with his Father we cannot guess. Already we have seen him preface his public mission with forty days of desert prayer. His proclamation of the new spirit and the choice of the twelve came only after a whole night on the mountainside. It was to a mountainside that he retreated again to prepare, with his Father, his revelation that he is the bread of life. And it is only after such prayer that he calls for his apostles' faith and fixes Peter's task in the kingdom. The gospels tell us no more than that Jesus prayed. Usually they stop right there, finishing the paragraph without a hint of what went on in those transcendent moments when God communed with God.

This is hardly surprising, however frustrating. What words would have sufficed? Furthermore, who would write them? The apostles and ourselves are left with little more than the basic object lesson that action in the kingdom is always the fruit of prayer. This is a great lesson, and one that—once forgotten or neglected—cripples our apostolic efforts. It is a plain fact that we must faithfully precede our acts with prayer. Still, this truth is not mysterious enough to explain those nights on the mountainside. Surely there is more to it than that.

And there is, but it is more than words can convey. When Jesus prays he seems to step clear out of the circle of humanity in order to be exclusively in that of his Father. In the Master there is a mysterious spiritual recess. It is a holy of holies to which even his mother had no approach, where only his Father was. There is a point in his human soul—the deepest, inmost point, wholly free of anything earthly or involved with worldly relations—which was solely dedicated to his Father. There is certainly a point like this in our own souls, and where we must retire in prayer to find ourselves alone with God.

But the Father to whom Jesus appeals belongs to him in quite a special sense. The Lord's act of prayer is utterly unique in that it occurs in the solitude of the Son with his Father. It is charged with the electric life-exchanges of the Trinity. At this altitude only the God-Man is at home. It is in such prayer that he is joined to the Father in an expressed one-ness in which no one, not even his disciples, can have a share. No wonder the apostles so often saw Jesus retreat alone for prayer; they were the moments when he could become most consciously himself.

No amount of companionship with Christ must ever lead us, through familiarity, to allow this sense of his overpowering divinity to diminish. If we are at all alert in our friendship with him, we must again and again be staggered with his mystery. He is God embodied. He welcomes us into warm friendship with himself, and it is in the deeply personal conversations of this friendship that our prayer consists. Our prayer consists in loving Jesus, thinking of him, being with him—with all the attention our souls can muster. But it must never lose that sense

of awesome wonder that we see in Jesus himself as he rever-
ences his Father. In prayer, faith assures us that we too com-
mune with God.

To give a glimpse of these inexpressible realities when
faith was hardly a week old in his apostles, Jesus selected Peter,
James and John to accompany him at prayer. It is one of the
two moments of his life on earth when man can watch the God-
Man at his private prayer (and the other one, at Gesthemane,
is exceedingly abnormal). This mountain of prayer to which the
Master brings the three apostles is far too high for them. However much they want to remain there, it is not for earthlings.
Yet because of it they will know him better. They will know
him really as he is, and be strengthened in the assurance that
this new level of conversation is real. For the Lord wants to
share himself with us entirely; he wants his joy to be our joy.

As soon as they were alone on the mountain top, he fell to
praying. "And even as he prayed," the scriptures tell us, "he
was transfigured in their presence; the fashion of his face was
altered, shining like the sun, and his garments became bright,
dazzling white as the light." The blinding grandeur of his
divinity gleamed through his outward appearance. The glory
of God was radiant in his humanity. His brilliance was beyond
words—a brilliance that belongs to him nonetheless, for he is
God. He is himself; nothing of his wonder now stands eclipsed,
so that men can see him as truly a man as well. And what blazing joy must have coursed through the humanity of Jesus at the
release of this restraint! There is nothing to restrain us from
supposing that such joy and such transfiguring beauty was the
Lord's on his other solitary trips to be with his Father alone.
But this is our only glimpse into the happiness he shares with
the Father.

Moses and Elias are there, the awakening apostles discover.

They hear enough of this heavenly conversation to tell us that Moses and Elias were speaking with Jesus about "the death which he was to achieve in Jerusalem." Nothing could have surprised the apostles then. Later on, though, it must have amazed them when they recalled that it was in such glory that the Cross was discussed. The grandeur of the moment in no way silenced the grave issues of the kingdom's foundation, for the very stuff of prayer is discussion—not just of God's glory, but of his will as well. It helps to see the Lord's coming sacrifice so thoroughly the subject of his prayer. In our faltering prayers it must also be so.

We think so much about God answering our prayers. We should be much more concerned with answering God's prayers, and seeking in prayer what he wants. We must accept the gravity of prayer; in it we, like Christ, receive our mission from God as well as the strength to accomplish it. And as it was with our Master, God's purposes for us are always marked with the grave but glorious sign of the cross.

Furthermore we know now where to bring the burdens of sorrow and evil that our world loads on us. Whatever our dismay, or however desperate our condition may seem, prayer clearly is the way we bring these crosses to Jesus. For we know we will encounter there the mystery of his suffering, and the mysterious meaning of our own. Hope issues from this confident access to Jesus, and recognition of further crosses that he and his Father may want us to bear.

Prayer is the meeting of the human personality with the divine. It meets in a great silence when all else is hushed, for God is speaking. And this is precisely what God does next at the transfiguration. Out of the cloud of light into which Moses and Elias had disappeared, comes the voice of God: "This is my beloved Son, in whom I am well pleased; to him, then, listen!"

The apostles hear God's voice with human ears; how greatly they fear! They know how utterly they are beyond their depth. It is Jesus who penetrates their fright with his touch. Soothingly, he tries to lift them out of their fear. They looked up to see only the Lord that they were used to. His prayer was over; again he was entirely with them.

It is abundantly clear to each of us that we cannot expect to reproduce the prayer of Christ in our lives. His is a prayer quite beyond the reach of simple man. Jesus sees and converses with the Father within the divine nature he himself possesses. There is no question of faith here, for faith can be no part of any action of the Lord; vision of the Father makes faith obsolete. But for us faith is the whole foundation of our prayer.

It is love of Jesus that must animate true prayer, but faith comes first; prayer can leap from no other fundament. True prayer is, after all, not natural to us. The three apostles realized it was good for them to be there, although they knew they did not belong in such high company at the transfiguration. This is not mere humility; they feared because they were drawn so far beyond their natural limits. Only in heaven can we look forward to prayer like the face-to-face prayer of Christ. While still on earth our condition is limited to being faithful. It is natural for Jesus to pray so; not for us.

Bewildered by the immensity of their great experience, Peter, James and John must at the same time have been greatly impressed by the honor it had been to be there. To what heights their Master had led them! They truly were members of God's family, citizens in no ordinary kingdom. To support their new faith he had given them this glimpse of its realities. These three would need all this support to bear the sight of Jesus as desolate in the garden of Gesthemane as he was radiant on Thabor.

We must not expect any of the physical or emotional joys

that Jesus knew in his prayer; we are much more likely to feel absolutely nothing. With the exception of his unusual night of prayer before his passion, the Master's prayer is not like ours in this respect. He did not share our aridity, our lack of response to divine contact. We are left to faith for assurance that God is with us when we talk to him. Our natural senses do not reach out into this supernatural world—only faith can enable us to focus on our listener. Left behind, our senses usually fall to seeking, distractedly, whatever objects they can find to fix on. All this we must accept as part of our life of faith, our real life with God without vision.

Yet the helps God gives us are such that a truly yearning faith can gradually come to make prayer as constant a part of our lives as it was for our Master. It takes discipline and desire, but we can hope to achieve a state where prayer is always occurring in us. Then, when we do find a moment to pray and do nothing else, it is as if, by removing a veil, we allow our inner awareness of God to occupy all our consciousness. To be so will be to be living, completely, a life of prayer. One would then constantly find himself wishing to return to God in full prayer as soon as he is free. And is not this state like that of our Lord who so yearned to be alone with his Father in prayer? And there on Thabor, did he not lift the veil that covered his glory all day to become truly himself?

Neither he nor we can remain on that mountain forever. A world surrounds us and calls on us. The scene that greets the four who come down the mountain from the transfiguration is in violent contrast with what they leave behind. The other apostles stand about in helpless dismay. Together with the crowd and the Scribes a few Pharisees are probably there tremendously enjoying their failure to help a frightfully sick boy. The boy's father has begun to lose confidence in the proceedings. Quickly Jesus extracts from the father the frightening account of his son's illness: hysterical epilepsy complicated by a devil. Then he calls for faith from the father and receives that marvelously honest answer that, I suppose, we all echo in times of strain, "Lord, I do believe; help my disbelief!" Then comes the cure. Faith, again, has made all things possible; the devil is ousted; all is well.

Where did we fail? ask the nine apostles whose usual methods of exorcism had proved useless. They had shown no faith. Up against an adversary greater than usual, they had not turned to God for help. The power they have is only on loan from above; this they seem to have forgotten. Remembering this, and pleading for God's help with all their might, would have turned the tide. As the Master explains, "There is no way of casting out such spirits as this except by prayer and fasting."

Effective prayer is total prayer, prayer where we put ourselves wholly into it. Fasting, self-denial, self-discipline—these are the hard means by which we gain sufficient possession of ourselves to be able to give ourselves completely to prayer. Then we have the detachment we need. Jesus has given us, and his twelve, sufficient warning that we can follow him only if we do in fact leave all else. This is eminently true of prayer as well. It takes all the courage and discipline he will help us to gain, if we ourselves yearn for them. Only with faith and real detachment can we focus ourselves directly on Jesus and be entirely absorbed in him.

Here again we face one problem Jesus did not know within himself: sin, personal sin. He never had to include in his words to his Father any plea for forgiveness for himself. Not so with us. Every approach to God's greatness reminds us of our failures; every prayer must include a personal *miserere*. Asking God's help in yanking out the affection for sin rooted in ourself, pleading for his help in curing these wounds—these are harsh tasks on our road to detachment. These evils within us are the devils that only prayer and fasting can cast out. And it seems the task is never done, so little is our faith.

From the midst of our struggles it is awe-inspiring for us dust-born creatures to look up and see Jesus at prayer. Then we see in what a glory of light the holiness of God flashes out from the soul of Jesus. He does not stand before his heavenly Father as a beggar, and still less as a prodigal son. He looks up at him with the untroubled, glowing eyes of a child and, as if it were the most natural thing in the world, unites himself with him in the most intimate personal communion.

Since prayer and sacrifice were first offered up on earth, never has anyone—saint or sinner—prayed like this.

IT IS ONLY A MATTER OF TIME BEFORE THE APOSTLES FIND THEIR OWN EFFORTS UNREWARDING AND TURN TO THEIR MASTER, ASKING HIM TO TEACH THEM HOW TO PRAY. It is a request that every one of us echoes. And he replies with a simplicity that astounds us, as it must have astounded the twelve. To be honest, it seems that he gives us precious little advice.

I would guess that most of us do not pray more because we feel we do not know how to pray, and this is what we expect Christ's reply to satisfy. We all suspect, perhaps, that there is some trick to it, some knack we do not have. We have tried to pray but nothing happened (we say to ourselves), as if we expected to feel some weird electric buzz. Or perhaps we have been looking and asking for some particular thing, and since God does not give us what we want we decide that our prayers are no good at all. We fall into the error of expecting some sort of slot machine answer to prayer—as if we have only to say our little prayer, pull the lever, and down comes the jackpot.

But does this sound very much like the way we would approach a Father who we know loves us? All this is corrected with the opening words of the model prayer, the Our Father, that Jesus offers us. If we have courage enough to place our prayers against the criterion he offers, do they not usually seem at least a bit selfish? Too often we pray like spoiled children, not like sons who love their Father and deeply know that he will always give them what they need and more. Our prayer must be a really personal act of faith that God *is* our Father, that he knows best what we need, that what we need most is what he needs, that his kingdom come, that his name be glorified, that his will be done. And when we simply say that we need him, that is real prayer. We need, above all, the daily bread he gives.

With the remainder of the Our Father we attend to our own outside needs: that we be at peace with all the rest of God's creatures, offending no one, forgiving all offenses, through his help and his delivery.

Is there not a somewhat incredible simplicity to all this? It does, to a degree, answer the apostles' question; but it seems to shed more light on what we are to pray for than on how we are to pray.

We can imagine the apostles restating their question. And amidst all our inadequacies at prayer, we too must ask for more direction. Again the answer the Master offers is astounding in its simplicity. All he has told them before should be enough. What is the parade of virtues he has already exposed to us? Humility, purity of heart, prudence, and above all, faith —are not these the basic ingredients of a truly prayerful attitude? Add to this a full awareness of the fact that God is as really a Father to us as he is to Jesus—is that not enough? To realize that he will attend to every need of his children with wisdom beyond what we could expect of any earthly father, is that not enough? Or are we expecting some key to enjoying prayer, to getting something out of it?

What Jesus does tell us about how we ought to pray *is* precious little, but it promises us everything. He commands that, in prayer, we must persevere. In fact, if we bring together all of our Lord's teaching on prayer, we find that it contains practically only one recommendation: perseverance. He repeats and repeats, and keeps coming back to the same subject with different parables, all bearing on the same theme: courageous perseverance. We are shamelessly to ask and ask and ask, to knock unremittingly. Prayer is a repeated act, an insistent, habitual act, that only becomes a true virtue when it is a real habit; when it is, first and faithfully, to the Father and to the Father's Son that we always look confidently for aid. This is the effect of more than sentiment; it can only result from a total commitment to the truth that God is our Father, that all depends on him. We must understand that this is the way in which he wants us to deal with him. It is almost superfluous to add that he will always answer, and always in the best way—not just "our way," for that would reveal him as a poor Father.

All this seems so rudimentary that at first one wonders whether there has not been some mistake. One would have expected something more "interesting." Perhaps the truth is too simple for us. But let us look the truth in the face. The Lord's urgent command on prayer was: keep trying, always keep praying. Prayer, after all, is not something we are to do to please ourselves. We pray to please God. Eloquence is not what he asks of us; it does not matter whether our prayer is fancy or high-flown. It is rather the attention we give God, our selfless, personal effort to please our Father and tell him simply that we love him. It might be said that in commanding us to

pray—especially us rushed twentieth-century Christians—Jesus
asks us to give his Father what we treasure most: our time, a
few minutes of our precious time. It is, after all, the vital characteristic of love that it compels our attention above all else.

To learn to pray, then, we must simply pray. We must pray
a great deal, and make ourselves keep starting over again even
if there is no response, even if there is no apparent result. Jesus
stressed perseverance as he did because he knew how difficult
it would be for us, because of our itch for novelty and change.
He insists that it should be enough for us to know that our
Father is waiting for us to pray, that he never stops wanting us
to pray, even when we have no wish to do so—perhaps even
especially then. Our attention to him is to be as unremitting as
his attention to us.

How ARE WE TO SUM ALL THIS UP? What is the framework for
these great truths? Simply that we, newly members in a kingdom that is heavenly, must now converse with our Lord and
God with prayer that is on this level. We are challenged to
pray with prayer that is great because our station is great, and
close to God—so close that we are really his children, and he
really our Father.

If our courage should falter at these heights it is not amazing; we are walking on the air of faith, and breathing only the
air of faith. It is solely on the word of Jesus that we are here;
no sight or feeling can be expected to comfort us. He will sustain us. Believing this wholeheartedly, we can pray with the
great confidence and simplicity of children curled up comfortably at the feet of their Father.

What marks then this man of prayer? An awareness, a
responsiveness, an active aliveness to the entire universe, visible and invisible. It is prayer that reveals, and makes real to

us, all of God's reality. It transfigures our sight of the world, and leads us to see all as it is in his wisdom. This is the great vision and composure we see in our Master, Jesus, master of prayer. And with great prayer are we not invited to join him in pleading with his Father and ours, that his kingdom come, that his will be done, in us as it is in heaven?

If it is precious little the Master tells us of prayer, it is all we need to know. No one has ever claimed—no one who followed him and his directions with unfailing courage—that he does not tell us enough. After all, we need only attend to him, and give all we have generously to Jesus.

For God has spoken, out of his cloud of glory: "This is my beloved Son, in whom I am well pleased; to him, then, listen!"

If we do listen we will learn from Jesus, the unique son of the Father, the urgency of prayer and what it is.

He knows. "To him, then, listen!"

6 FORGIVENESS AND MERCY

The Scene Shifts

THE QUIET APOSTOLATE IN GALILEE IS COMING TO A CLOSE. It bears small but essential fruit. Many foundation stones for the kingdom have been laid. Its shape is clear now. Jesus will be its head with a human vicar, Peter, at his side. The basic credential of its every citizen is faith, faith that will invigorate prayer, prudence and purity of heart in every believer.

This idyllic gentleness cannot be the whole story. As soon as it can be borne by his disciples Jesus begins to inculcate a startling new trend. This Lord of theirs—whom they recognize now as God-man—is to be slain. He is a redeemer, a sacrificial lamb, a victim-priest. He wants faith in him to be objective and inclusive. All have heard happily of the goal Jesus promises: life, eternal blessedness and joy. Now is revealed the providential, and unbelievable, means to this end.

"Remember this well," the Master warns them, "the Son of Man is to be given up into the hands of men. With much ill-usage they will put him to death, and he will rise again after three days." Again and again, the gospels tell us, Jesus repeated this dire prophecy, so at variance with Jewish hopes. Such forebodings stun the apostles. And they refuse to believe that this end could be his. They seem never to get beyond balking at the cruel passion foretold; the resurrection will come as a complete surprise. They fail to look beyond the horror. They miss the chance to see "how it was fitting that the Christ should undergo these sufferings and so enter into his glory." Yet they will begin to understand that the promised new life is purchased by death. The kingdom they will administrate is to be enlivened and nourished by sacrifice.

To weather all these storms they will need all the virtue they have gained. His cross will be a cross for them too. Self-importance has no place here. They must make little of themselves as children sometimes do. They must learn to renounce themselves, to forget themselves, to erase themselves from their primary consideration. Jesus asks this quality of us if we would seek true greatness.

It is the redeemer's task that is now emphasized, and the enemy of redemption is sin. If someone spreads sin's gospel he is the enemy's agent, and one better off were he anchored in the sea to drown. "Woe to the world, for the hurt done to consciences . . . and woe to the man through whom it comes!"

The consequences of sin are so enormous that to picture them Jesus points to the torments of hell. There "the worm which eats never dies, the fire is never quenched." Is this vivid enough to illustrate the gravity of sin?

Hell, given this graphic reality, commands an explanation. And none is found but the immense majesty of God. No tragedy, no affront, can be imagined that can compare with that of offending God. Rejection of God is the sum of evil; he does not reign then as the ultimate goal of all our labors. Discarding God to look elsewhere we can find only hell. It is hell to be without him.

The lesson is clear. For the apostles and for every man the choice is unmistakable. It is sin, not God, that must be rejected. It is all else, not God, which is to be discarded, if it blocks our path to him. It is better to enter into the kingdom maimed than not at all. No compromise is possible here; we cannot have both sin and God for masters. On this point Jesus—and all who follow him—must always be intolerant.

Renunciation is pointed out to us as a basic attitude we are to have in facing sin. Great things are asked of us in the name of renunciation; Jesus will renounce even his human urge to self-preservation. And all this is because of sin; its cost, without repentance, is eternal.

It may be puzzling, therefore, to note how the Lord here introduces us to his feelings towards the sinner. The ninety-nine sheep in no need of forgiveness are deserted while he sets out after the one that strays. Furthermore, its discovery is cause for a burst of divine pleasure that outshines the fidelity of the faithful ninety-nine. Clearly, there is a fundamental distinction to be made: our reaction to the sinner is to be different from our reaction to his sin. The time for judgment has not come yet; our Lord will be a shepherd now. We are living out our time of trial and, while that lasts, mercy will master justice.

Forgiveness presupposes renunciation. To be capable of forgiveness that is genuine we must overcome so much. Towards anyone that offends us our reaction is, very naturally, one of hostility. Natural animosity is one of our inbred defenses. When the injury done is quite personal resentment quickly arises, a personal development of hostility. It is not so much a general reaction to danger that triggers hostility. More intimate still, it is our honor or our position that is challenged.

Up springs the desire for revenge. To retaliate would restore our self-respect by humiliating the offender. We want retribution; we claim the eye for an eye; we ourselves are going to administer justice; at least inwardly, we take the law into our own hands.

Is this not a true graph of our human reactions to an offense? To a "sin" against ourselves? Once an injury is done this set of natural mechanisms begins to work in us, and all in a direction opposed to forgiveness. Furthermore, who can deny that "revenge is sweet," that there is not satisfaction in teaching the other fellow a lesson? These are natural pleasures to be sure—and limited, sour and selfish to boot—but real and personal tendencies of our natures all the same.

The need for true renunciation is plain if we are to forgive truly and fully. Here we must deny ourselves. It is this bundle of defensive instincts that we must discard, forgetting ourselves. It is no easy task. See the real danger that exists for the forgiver, because his effort is surrounded by traps full of self-satisfaction. He must be well equipped with self-denial, and a sharp eye for any deflection from his selfless goal.

The apostles have frequently witnessed this complete absence of animosity in Jesus as he forgives. There is a magnanimity about him that renders his forgiveness soothing and acceptable to the sinner. With no personal bias intruding, the peace he confers has no harsh edge. It is totally merciful; it exacts no revenge.

We are asked to achieve this high degree of poise. However sharply intolerant we must be to the sin, the sinner and his repentance can be met with loving forgiveness. This composure needs to be deeper than the bridling urge to be hostile. It takes courage to counteract this belligerent wariness, a courage that can only spring from a deep sense of intimate security. Similarly, the itch for revenge is only quelled if we possess an intrinsic honor within us that we know is invulnerable to external offense. This all comes to a head when we are able to relinquish the wish to see punishment meted out. To give up this satisfaction is to give up our delightful sense of superiority towards the sinner. We climb off the judgment seat and come down to the sinner's level as a sharer of a common fate. This is, of course, where all of us belong—for all of us surely are sinners.

Our pretence of complete goodness is one we tightly cling to when faced with an offender other than ourselves. Indeed, to discover most sympathetically how real is the distinction between the sin and the sinner, we just need to recall how thoroughly we apply it to our own selves. The problem, then, is giving someone else this same benefit we confer on ourselves so lovingly. A selfless and difficult task to be sure—and one Jesus will have to return to again and again as essential to true forgiveness.

At this moment, however, Jesus is broadly introducing the twelve to characteristics of the true shepherds he wants them to be. They are to be devoted, undistracted, unselfish shepherds. They are to care for the little ones of his flock; to cherish the weak; to pursue the strayed with a shepherd's concern. They are to be at great pains to make it easy to repent; privately is best. Public humiliation is not to be sought for that is to extract out of forgiveness all the love that makes it Christian. What the Lord gives—and what we must give—is forgiveness that is, at the same time, merciful.

Why has elaborate treatment been given to this point? All this is but prelude to a tremendous announcement. This forgiveness that Jesus gives, the twelve are also to give in his name. The Lord proclaims that they will bind and loose as he does, with his power. They are to be administrators of his mercy. For those who cannot come to him, Christ leaves lieutenants empowered to forgive in his stead. "Who can forgive sins but God, and God only?" the Pharisees asked. They had never envisioned this possibility: that God would let man dispense power that was strictly divine.

This was thoroughly clear to Peter. The problem of sin and forgiveness was personally vivid to his honest nature. He ventures a delicate question, conscious of his primary position in this distribution of God's mercy. Delicacy is hardly one of Peter's obvious traits yet, for all his bluster, not an example exists in the gospels where Peter fails to give genuine compassion to all in need. This is because he knows his own need and his own difficulty. He asks Jesus how often must one forgive a repentant brother—"as much as seven times?" His remark is in perfect taste; humanly he is being very generous. After repeated offenses—even two or three—how grudging does our forgiveness become? Peter doubtless showed an openness Jesus loved, but it needed to be brought to perfection. It is a superhuman mercy, a divine forgiveness that Peter and the eleven will administer.

"I tell you," the Master stresses in reply, "to forgive not seven wrongs, but seventy times seven!" For the truly sorry God's mercy is infinite. It is to be dealt out in no human measure, however generous. What an awesome task it is to become an outlet for divine mercy. No apostle must ever cramp God's generosity. God gives as he wishes, not as we wish.

It is to this subject that the Lord then addresses himself. There is a condition attached to God's pardon. It has already been made an element of the model prayer—forgive us as we forgive those offending us.

It is through a scene of staggering ingratitude that Jesus seeks to expose this truth so graphically that no one can mistake it. A master, about to cast into debtors' prison a servant guilty of immense debt, is moved with pity and forgives him. The amount of his indebtedness is so monstrous that it is immediately apparent that God is the master and sin the offense. God's beneficence shines before our eyes. And underlined, too, is the profligate cost of sin. The sinner kneels prostrate before such consequences, pleading without right for mercy, and mercy is done.

Who can forget what this forgiven servant does, then, to a fellow servant guilty of a debt literally thousands of times less? Malice replaces mercy; the greatly blessed becomes small beyond measure. Ingratitude like this is almost inconceivable. How can it be? Instead of mercy continued, we witness an explosion of selfish glee, unforgiving and cruel.

Could that servant have had any true gratitude? He did not regard his immense debt as really his own. Otherwise his gratitude would have measured his release. He had explained away his guilt; decided he had a right to pardon; justified himself. When mercy came, all his selfish reasonings shouted that they had been right all along; that he owed nothing to his master, not even gratitude. He was not like the rest of men.

The rest of men turn on him, as does even the merciful master, and justice is done because mercy has had no effect. The solemn conclusion Jesus intones is this: "Thus my heavenly Father will deal with you, if brother does not forgive brother with all his heart."

Repentance must be a wholly honest act. It must be an unflinchingly whole recognition of wrong in us. More than this, we must face the wrong done to others as our responsibility. Perhaps this unforgiving servant is not so incomprehensible. There are seeds of false penitence in each of us. Yet falsity seldom gets as fully out of control as in that ungrateful servant. Most of us would have been up to forgiving the tiny debt after such a windfall, but even that might be just a grand gesture, not forgiving our bother "with all our hearts."

The key to repentance that is true is also the key to true forgiveness for others. Deep, thorough insight into the greatness of God—the God whom we callously offend, who is so magnificently good to us—this is the key to giving forgiveness and repentance the grave urgency they require. The Lord must have this acceptance of himself and his Father as fearful great, for otherwise God is not recognized. Without it how can he forgive us, for we lack religion? If sin is nothing of moment neither is mercy.

If, on the other hand, we admit our guilt and deal with others remembering our own need and how God has blessed us with his mercy, how greatly God loves us. We are fulfilling the only condition to God's forgiveness: that we remember how great is our need for it, and that we have caused this need ourselves.

It is easy to see why Jesus warned that forgiveness of our brothers should precede prayer. If we are full of grudges, our unforgiveness will step in between us and the Father and smother our prayer. We will have forgotten again who we are, sinners. Our hearts are closed hearts, then, that have shut out remembrance of their own wrongs and stand dishonest before God.

A heart that is open and clean—how often has Jesus called Galilee to this simple perfection! For eighteen months Christ's homeland has been a tabernacle for God teaching and acting publicly. Its time has come and gone; Galilee will not see Jesus again. All that Christ has offered has been ignored with colossal ingratitude. How sad the responsibility for spurning so much. Its native son utters tragic words as he leaves; they are as heavy with doom as those Jerusalem will come to hear. Galilee's destiny is desolation and ruin, and one of its own choosing.

Galilee did not need Jesus. To deny our sinful state is to

insult God and to declare our salvation unnecessary. Even Sodom was not so self-satisfied, the Master recalls. Pagan Tyre and Sidon were not so self-sated that they felt no need for God's mercy. Forgiveness can only be given to the forgiver, and Galilee asked for none of it.

He knows when he isn't wanted, and leaves. It is truly a mark of human greatness to see refusal and recognize it without bitterness. Jesus saw that he could do no more. But with what sorrow he must have regarded their failure.

JERUSALEM WILL REPULSE HIM LESS GENTLY. Sin, there, will be a violent foe. Everything about Jerusalem bears the odor of combat and the enemy is ever on the attack. The kingdom of this world welcomes only its own.

Jesus comes to save; he shares in the world's sorrow so that he may cure it. Of opposite mind, our urge is to escape mankind's suffering. We tend to deny our part in it. Christ's very presence is an affront to this. Jerusalem is painfully reminded of its debt. The Pharisees grope about for a prop for their complacency. They will not confess themselves to be as other men, sinners, and neither must Jesus.

They want to force the Master to judge as they do. An adulteress is dragged into his presence, fresh from her sin. The legal zealots proclaim that the law prescribes stoning, and then, tauntingly, ask judgment from Jesus. "What is your sentence?" they ask again. Jesus is doodling in the sand, ignoring the captious question. As they continue to persist, the Master finally retorts quietly with a sentence that is deafening: "Whichever one of you is free from sin shall cast the first stone at her."

As Jesus again writes quietly on the sand the great silence is marked only by the slow shuffling of feet. Was it the veiled threat of further embarrassment, first understood by the elders, that moved them? Or, for once, had the Master succeeded in touching the coated fibers of their hearts? In any case they fell back in retreat. They had failed to make Jesus like themselves.

Without such a fierce reminder how easy it is to cast the first, second or third stone, especially the second or third. It is hard to retain unflinchingly a true view of sin and ourselves. How much easier to cover our sins with the cosmetics of self-esteem, and to stone those others that we catch with the cosmetic off. If it is false at all, piety is as full of pitfalls as impiety.

All the accusers have scurried off. Jesus addresses the adulteress—still standing there—with respect, "Woman . . . has no one condemned you? Neither shall I, but sin no more." The sinner, when contrite, is respected and loved; the sin reproved.

To render forgiveness acceptable and "win" your brother, show no sign of righteous indignation. This hostility blocks true pardon's effect. Indignation is often the mask that hides condescension, smirking ethical superiority, even pharisaical presumption!

It is a different sort of search that our Lord makes for sinners. He hunts them with a shepherd's care. So also must the shepherds that follow in his stead. The apostles especially must learn how to make his forgiveness merciful, never bristling with judgment. They will bear his power to forgive. They are to become shepherds, whose coming the keeper of the sheepfold will welcome. The sheep will be attentive to their voices. But they must be recognized, not as strangers, but as shepherds who know their sheep. If there is any hint that they have come to plunder or punish, the sheep will scatter. They must be known to the sheep as their protectors in order to make the mercy they bear acceptable, to make it love conferred.

The shepherd is one with his flock. He is not apart, superior or stinting in his care. He seeks no escape from his involvement; he loves it. Peter and his band are to be stand-ins for the good shepherd. All the warmth Jesus brings to this task must be theirs. To forgive is to accept another's fault as one's own.

Full understanding of this whole matter of forgiveness, and its personal cost, is so necessary to each of them—as well as each of us. Anything less will be to risk not only being characterized as a hireling, but misunderstanding a fundamental purpose of our Lord's coming among us.

"I am the good shepherd," he tells us, ". . . . and for these sheep I am laying down my life." Here at last appears the answer to the question that has been lying under all our discussion: how is this forgiveness to be effected? Sin's price will be paid by the ignominy and death Jesus has foretold. Sin is not forgotten—it calls for atonement. To forgive is to accept another's faults as one's own, and this Jesus accepts as his mission. For this his Father has sent him.

He assures us that "no one can rob him of" his life, he is laying it down of his own free accord. He is himself to be not only our forgiver, but also the gift which gains it. Our shepherd God promises to be our sacrificial lamb with no trace of superiority but only obedient love. He wills to be the lamb of God who takes away the sins of the world and grants us peace.

The sacrificial plan stands revealed. Its goal is full peace, not a synthetic tranquillized peace gained by ignoring sin. The seventy-two disciples go out to announce its coming, and the Master accredits them, saying, "He who listens to you, listens to me!" To every household he bids them wish peace. This is to become the whole function of his Church and its every member: to bring to all this pastoral peace the good shepherd earns.

We have made great strides, strides toward and into Jerusalem, into the unfolding themes of our redemption's accomplishment. The demands on the apostles are new and many. The struggle with darkness is joined, and they cannot see beyond it. They do not notice Jesus saying that he is laying down his life "to take it up again afterwards." They overlook the depth of Christ's joy as he exclaims, on the return of the seventy-two disciples, "I watched while Satan was cast down like a lightning flash from heaven!"

But they understand clearly enough the gravity of their mission. The difficulty and importance of forgiveness is too real a problem for every man to be overlooked. And their whole destiny, indeed the destiny of forgiveness for all mankind, is more absolutely centered on Jesus, their friend and shepherd. Imagine then, how in the midst of their growing fright of the Pharisees, with their faith and numbers small, with their sense of personal sin and inadequacy heightened, how full of comfort and promised forgiveness were these thrilling words from their friend:

> Come to me, all you that labor and are burdened; I will give you rest. Take my yoke upon yourselves, and learn from me; I am gentle and humble of heart; and you shall find rest for your souls. For my yoke is easy, and my burden light.

7 FORTITUDE

Jerusalem Conflict

A SENSE OF DESTINY IS IN THE AIR. The scent of combat is in the wind, becoming gradually more intense and gripping. God's plan of salvation is emerging more clearly, more ominously, more enormously. Into the central arena of Israel—already electric with conjecture and suspense—strides Jesus. He is a Jesus unleashed, unrestrained, his every word and act crackling with personal power.

Two groups stand by watching tensely. The Pharisees who oppose him strain to hear any phrase they can twist into sedition. Their guarded muttering among themselves betrays their increasing and anxious animosity. The other group is the apostles, anxious also. What will be the outcome of this direct, frontal assault the Master launches? He is always surprising, always provoking their minds to grander awareness of how immense are the truths they hear. But they stand uneasy and fearful before the glares of the Pharisees. These are among the acknowledged leaders of the Jews, learned and powerful; can twelve plain Jewish fishermen stand easily against them?

No indifference is apparent now in the audiences who hear Jesus. With sure consciousness of his aim, the Lord commands their decision. He is a man of clear will, showing no hesitation, no reversal of statement, no vacillation. His every act and every word is sharp-edged with firmness. Indeed, it is always with awe that we watch the heroic. And the resolute virility and fixity of purpose with which Jesus sees his Father's will as his appointed task, and carries it through despite all obstacles, is in truth heroic.

"Whereupon Jesus cried aloud as he taught in the temple, 'I have not come on my own errand, I was sent by one who has a right to send; and him you do not know. I know him [the Father], because I come from him; it was he who sent me.'" As he will emphasize again and again, it is God's errand he comes on, not his own; he seeks no credit for himself. Yet many would seize the Lord for the claim he has made. To *know* God! —this man has claimed something superhuman, something blasphemous! And so the Pharisees quickly send out their police to arrest Jesus.

Courageous is the word for Jesus here in the midst of Jerusalem's dangers, but as a word it does not go deep enough. What is occurring is more than bravado, more than valor, more than nerveless bravery. Of such is pagan heroism compounded. Christian courage is a sign of sanctity, not of a merely human daring. The exterior element of the deed plays its necessary part, of course, but what gives to Christian fortitude its intense strength is not a person's natural courage, but the knowledge that he has strength beyond his own. He is not counting on himself. He is not on his own errand.

Again the Master's voice rings out, this time at the very climax of the feast: "If any man is thirsty, let him come to me, and drink; yes, if a man believes in me, as the scripture says,

'Fountains of living water shall flow from his bosom!' " With these strangely compelling words, foreseeing the Holy Spirit's seal on his work, Jesus has pointed out himself as the source of spiritual life—and still he is not arrested.

"Nobody has ever spoken as this man speaks," explain the police returning empty-handed. But this were better left unsaid, for it angers their Pharisee masters. They rage at police and people, finally exhibiting their complete contempt for that damnable pack, "these common folk, who have no knowledge of the law." Nicodemus, the one of them who knows something of Jesus, bravely tries to check them, but it is hard to talk sense in a general mood of scorn, and he too ends up insulted.

Men can become so absorbed in some spiritual scheme as to make not only things but other men subservient to it, making mere tools of them for the furtherance of their own purposes. Thus this group of the Pharisees; for them the "common folk" do not count; they care nothing for others' individual needs, or rights, or happiness. No, it is the law, the ideal, the general, that is everything. These are the spiritual bullies; bullies in pursuit, they would claim, of a spiritual ideal. Such hypocrisy, so well entrenched, grants them great self-righteousness. It gives them a false fortitude.

Again Jesus challenges their supposed pre-eminence: "I am the light of the world," he declares, "he who follows me can never walk in darkness; he will possess the light which is life." How this must have irked those Pharisees who claimed this position for themselves. Their response is measured: "You are testifying on your own behalf, your testimony is worth nothing."

The Master overrides this objection with a powerful statement of his own authority. Full self-knowledge does give one's self-testimony full value. His self-judgment is not like theirs, he points out fiercely, and what is more, the Father supports him, a Father of whom they have no knowledge if they deny his Son.

Fearful power, for good or for evil, is in the hands of those who know who they are, or merely think they do. Here we have a collision between both, the strength of each being clear and committed, each vibrantly convinced of his own rightness, our Lord rightly, the others falsely. It is obvious, all the same, that true courage and real force proceed from knowing not only who one is but also from whence, from whom. For our Lord, it is clear, his deepest strength comes from realizing fully that he is the Father's envoy and can count on the Father's strength.

The charge he lays to them is peremptory: "You will die with your sins upon you unless you come to believe that it is myself you look for." What else is the Master saying but that he must be the object, the very focal point, of all our religious energies? The whole thrust of our spiritual effort must be directed towards him. "Who are you, then?" ask the Jews captiously. Exasperated by such persistent ignorance Jesus exclaims, "What, that I should be speaking to you at all?" Men cannot play games with God's messenger. Men cannot stall and cavil when God speaks. One day they will understand, to their shame, who he is, when men "have lifted up the Son of Man" on the cross. Those who hear and learn what Jesus teaches in time will possess a truth that will set them free. Such was the faith Abraham had, but all who refuse this message from God can never claim to be sons of Abraham. "You belong to your father," the Master points out scathingly, but this father is "the devil, and you are eager to gratify the appetites which are your father's." They show all the marks of the devil, falsehood and murder. After all, are they not now plotting to kill him?

There is angry vituperation; men in the mob mouth curses and accusations. The air is charged with rage. And through it cuts the fierce challenge of Jesus, "Can any of you convict me of sin?" If not, he is supremely worthy of credence. Sprung from God, he brings God's truth—one they ignore because there is no godliness in them! They are someone else's sons.

How many men today are no one's sons! Wayward, fretful, excitable and miserable—these are the characteristics of empty men acting without final purpose. All their energy ends in final failure. Independence that repudiates God's fatherhood is bondage to sin and the devil's service. Man's strength is not to be spent in such frustration.

Having been so thoroughly "told off," the authorities retort with an atrocious affront, "We are right, surely, in saying that you are a Samaritan, and are possessed." It is God's own Son they so accuse! How must Jesus have shuddered with dismay at such a gross misunderstanding. It does not, however, deflect him from his purpose. Christian fortitude is fortitude that recoils before nothing. His courage is unflinching. "I am not possessed," he replies evenly; "it is because I reverence my Father that you have no reverence for me." And, what is more, "If a man is true to my word, to all eternity he will never see death!"

In the face of such bitter opposition Jesus steadfastly defends the honor of his Father. Yet the bile of the crowd is overflowing; such intensity must reach its violent outlet. And so it does.

To the taunt that he can hardly have seen Abraham the Lord delivers a claim that, in its immensity, reverberates yet in our ears: "Believe me, before ever Abraham came to be, I am!" He has bared his eternal origin. It is as explicit a claim to divinity as was the other such claim made out of a burning bush. More than enough to ignite tempers already ragged with anger, violence finally erupts. Those who hear him would kill

Jesus then and there. Stones are grabbed, arms are cocked. But their target is gone; in the climactic confusion the Master has calmly slipped away.

Hardly a week passes before another incident occurs. Jesus is reported to have cured, on the Sabbath, a man blind from birth. The fortunate man is hauled before Pharisees who seem to feel he is, in fact, unfortunate. Yet so jittery are they that they even begin to fight among themselves. This altercation is calmed by the appearance of the blind man's parents, who are more frightened still. Bullying these parents restores pharisaical courage, and again they go to work on the man who has gained sight. But his courage knows no faltering; he draws the conclusion none want to hear: Jesus is God's spokesman.

It is a magnificent contest—sophistry versus insight. Finally, in a burst of daring, the erstwhile blindman tries to make these Pharisees see. In their defeat they can only answer with insults. Recrimination and heated abuses—these are the unmistakable signs of a poor loser. And the man is cast out from their presence.

The Lord cannot let such courage go unrewarded. He completes the man's cure by inviting and accepting his belief. "I have come into this world," Jesus tells him, "that a sentence may fall upon it, that those who are blind should see, and those who see should become blind." These ubiquitous Pharisees pounce on this statement. "Are we blind, too?" they ask. A crushing, chilling answer comes to this sarcastic question: only those who will admit sickness seek a cure. Pharisaical blindness is a blindness Jesus is not permitted to cure. They claim he has no power; that leaves him no room to act.

We have been given a clear view of the inner workings of these authorities and their bullying, false use of power. And once we have understood this much of their character, we can foresee there is little chance for Christ. Tragedy is inevitable.

Our Lord, however, is gaining a hearing. Simple folk are flocking to him. So into the din of battle comes a moment of joy. "Filled with gladness," Jesus exults, "O Father, Lord of heaven and earth, I give you praise that you have hidden all this from the wise and prudent, and revealed it to little children!" His strength is for the weak only, only for those who see its need.

At their next encounter with the Master the Pharisees are more cautious. He turns their questions back on them and one of them is forced to recite the two great commandments from Deuteronomy: that God is to be loved with our whole heart, our whole soul, our whole mind, and our whole strength; and our neighbor as ourself. God is to be served with vigor, with the strength of the whole person. Such fortitude is a manly virtue that is more than manly, for it rests finally in the impetus of divine love. Beyond strength of arm or will, it is the full strength of the soul which is required.

Then, to cover the simplicity of his answer, the Pharisee responds with a further question: "Who is my neighbor?" Christ's reply is the deceptively simple tale of the good Samaritan. However beautiful, it has in it harsh indictment for these religious rulers, who are compared unfavorably with their despised neighbors, the Samaritans. It takes courage to expose oneself in kindness to another; this is not the way of these wary Pharisees. Theirs is the preference for the spectacular public act. Much more fortitude is needed for the little unseen act; indeed, its proof is often most spectacular if it is worked out through small daily fidelities. This makes it most clear that it is God's honor that one is working for, not one's own. The question's answer is now apparent: we are obliged to love everyone in need, Jew or Samaritan, friend or enemy. With this subtle stroke Jesus has entirely superseded any complicated rabbinical casuistry.

This is a scene of prepossessing charm on our Lord's part. It is, furthermore, important to notice how carefully Jesus uses this charm. Never is it employed to deprive anyone of his liberty, to force a decision. The Master refuses himself any means which captivates a person, even when an individual is unaware of it, for he knows that God is thus deprived of the only thing which has any worth for him. No ability, no strength, no trick, must ever attempt to replace grace. This is why Jesus always waits for his subject to give him an opening. Truly, the use of fortitude can be delicate and dangerous, so easy is it to begin to dominate, not direct.

If fortitude is true, however, it bears with it a sense of certain victory. If God wills this work, and lends his strength to it, how can one be less than certain that it will succeed? It was with this sureness that the Lord must have accepted an invitation to dine with one of the Pharisees. He is not overawed by his enemies; he somehow seems to defy their reality.

The meal is going peacefully until the familiar pharisaical hypocrisy rears its head. This triggers from our Lord an absolutely fearsome and pitiless indictment of their faults. Right in their midst, in private with his antagonists, the Master upbraids them in a manner so scathing that one trembles with fear for them. "All running with avarice and wickedness," they are "whitened sepulchres"; they are murderers; they are even sadists, loading men "with burdens too heavy to be borne." Small wonder that, "after he left the house, they resolved to hunt him down mercilessly." A "small" man shamed makes a vindictive and unscrupulous enemy.

What has come over the Lord; whence this audacity? We can only say that God's power moved him to it. Indeed, once the unrest of Christ has been let into a man's heart, he often becomes incomprehensible and a cause for scandal, especially among Pharisees.

To his apostles, who will have to contend with the Pharisees of ages to come, warning is given publicly. "Have nothing to do with the leaven of the Pharisees," he says, "it is all hypocrisy." It is a constant human danger; we must be alert to it and unafraid before it. However insidious it is, we must be sure that we have strength to overcome it, if it is God's true strength we use. Fortitude is the virtue that enables us to face undismayed all the dangers which stand in the way of the execution of our duty. It restrains rashness and conquers fear.

To conquer fear . . . will fear vanish? Hardly; what is involved is not the absence of fear but its control. "Do not be afraid of those who can kill the body, and after that can do no more," Jesus instructs us. Fear only the loss of eternal life. And even then God watches over us with a care that counts every hair, a care so special that we should be fully assured; nothing need perplex us.

"Whoever acknowledges me before men, I too will acknowledge him before my Father." The Master too will support us if we faithfully seek to be as courageous as he is. It is this heroic spirit, this unconditional staking of our lives for the known truth, that he demands. Disciples of his must be so valiant, so resolutely purposeful. We have gifts which are ours by nature and the wonderful gifts he will add. We must blend all these into strength like his, a manly Christian strength.

Apostles can expect no better treatment than their Master; their fortitude will be as tested as his. They will be dragged before judges for trial; there is no persecution they will not know. Then it will be for fortitude to provide the power to sustain, to endure. Then there will be none of the supporting ardor that comes with being on the attack. Or, even worse, the day will come when it will take great fortitude to struggle with that most indefinite of enemies, a faithless world. Then moral courage will find its role in urging us to mount above the dead level of average Christianity towards a life that fully depends on God's strength.

No idle speculations these; time is short. The final encounter of Christ's Judean ministry is about to occur; the final pattern of things is ominously emerging. With stirring force Jesus cries out: "It is fire that I have come to spread over the earth!" Already, the apostles can see, the blaze is kindling. Yet their Master will give them yet another great object lesson in courage.

Gathered around the Lord, the Jews cry out, "How long will you keep us in suspense? If you are the Christ, tell us openly." And he does. Into the face of their sure anger he speaks the claim he values most: "My Father and I are one!" One and the same unique God, one-natured and inseparable! Equally potent, one in strength, one in divinity, one in majesty!

Blasphemy! The shout goes out, stone him! The crowd falls into a pious rage; stones in hand, they are about to stone Jesus to death. Somehow, through this storm of wrath, the voice of the Master checks their onslaught.

Their passion-blinded eyes see him standing there composed and unafraid. Clearly his voice inquires, "My Father has enabled me to do many deeds of mercy in your presence, for which of these are you stoning me?"

For none of them, retorts the crowd, but "because you, who are a man, pretend to be God!"

Back comes the calm response: "Will you call be a blasphemer because I have told you I am the Son of God? If you find that I do not act like the son of my Father, then put no trust in me; but if I do, then let my actions convince you where

I cannot." And to this Jesus adds again his claim, "so you will recognize and understand that the Father is in me, and I in him."

In the face of death he has challenged them again to belief in him. Again he has spoken what they term blasphemy, but their reaction is not as grave, they only seek to seize him. The crowd is stirred, wondering, remembering all that had happened, recalling all that Jesus has done.

He leaves the question, so alive, in their minds, and leaves town. Jerusalem, the holy city, living heart of all Israel, has been visited for the last time before the end. The fig tree has but one more chance to bear fruit.

The conclusion to our observation of these conflicts in Jerusalem is shockingly clear: great force, great fortitude, must be ours in following Jesus. We must spend every energy in being like him; our every power will be called for. We must, indeed, "love the Lord our God . . . with our whole strength."

For there was a man that said to the Master, "Lord, is it only a few that are to be saved?"

And the answer Jesus gave him was simply: "Fight your way in at the narrow door!"

8 PIETY: FATHER AND SON

Travelling Perea

JESUS HAS DESERTED JERUSALEM, SCENE OF MORTAL COMBAT. "Today and tomorrow and the next day," he tells those who inquire, "I must go on my journeys"; but he will return for "there is no room for a prophet to meet his death, except at Jerusalem."

After the intensity of Judea, with its open strife and crises, with its urgent, angry tones, we are struck by the change of pace. Jesus is out of town now, teaching again with a serenity and simplicity that takes us back to Galilee. He has felt the soaring temperature of events and he adjusts. The end is already on the calendar: the Passover, in Jerusalem. The Master will use the meantime in completing lessons his disciples must learn.

As recorded in the gospels this period is one enjoying no apparent chronology of events, yet all the discourses of Jesus center on one immense theme. He would tell us more of his Father and his total care for us. And the extent to which we, as sons, must respond to his great goodness will emerge ever more clearly.

"I say to you, then," the Lord begins, "do not fret over your life, how to support it with food and drink; over your body, how to keep it clothed. Is not life itself a greater gift than food, the body than clothing?" The good God who has given us the greater—our bodies and our lives—will certainly not withhold from us the lesser. "See how the birds of the air never sow, or reap, or gather grain into barns, and yet your heavenly Father feeds them; have you not an excellence beyond theirs?"

This is a burst of earnest eloquence, but does it waft us away from reality with all its harsh needs, towards a land without anxieties? There is a condition upon which this providence hinges. The Master is not advising us not to be anxious about anything; be anxious, indeed, he tells us, but about the things that matter. These other things are not of everlasting importance.

"Do not fret, then, asking 'What are we to eat? or What are we to drink? or How shall we find clothing?' It is for the heathen to busy themselves over such things; you have a Father in heaven who knows that you need them all. Make it your first care to find the kingdom of God, and his approval, and all these things shall be yours without the asking!"

Our Lord is urging us most vividly to realize the unquestioned primacy we must give to God and his goals. To do this is to put ourselves in order, to have a hierarchy of value that God can recognize and support. All the same, this is not the heart of the matter.

The announcement that should move us most is so simple: "You have a Father in heaven," a Father who knows that you need all these things, a Father who will, so minutely, care for you. The distant and awesome view of God almighty that heathens must view is gone. With bounding heartbeat we see instead no dread God but a Father lovingly anxious to make every provision for us. His meticulous care for all he has made waves banner-like in every daisy field; his eye is on the sparrow, every one. To this our Lord subjoins exultantly, "Have you not an excellence beyond theirs?"

This is a truth that faith readily accepts—and with joy—yet too often leaves unrealized. God the Father's complete providence over us individually at every moment—do we not usually leave this truth in the category of baby-talk? Do we dismiss this casually as one of our birthrights, remembered only in an emergency when all else fails? Jesus would have us know him as our first resort.

And with what colossal inattention do we reward this Father's unremitting watch! Perhaps it is some childish conception of God's care that has crumbled within us. What a child asks and expects is immediate and pleasant deliverance from his difficulties. Not so what God's child may expect. Rather, he knows that his Father will provide him with all the means to overcome whatever obstacles block progress towards him, but in the way that he knows is best. This is the mature child's surrender to his Father's wisdom, admitting that God knows us better than we do.

The overwhelming fact remains: we have God for a Father. No good behavior on our part has earned this benefit. This is a Father who can see promise in one who has shown none. This is a Father who loves infinitely. This is our Father.

We must not try to make him over to suit ourselves. This is what has happened when one of us objects to God the Father admitting to his heaven some sinner who barely turned to him at the last moment. Would we tell this Father that he cannot be as fatherly as he wants? Could we wish to limit this Father's generosity?

To this attitude Jesus addressed the parable of those

laborers in a vineyard that worked, some of them, all day and others just an hour or two. Each received what was promised to those who had first come. No injustice was done, but those who had worked more were outraged. Our Lord recounts the answer they received: "Take what is your due . . . ; it is my pleasure to give as much to this late-comer as you. Am I not free to use my money as I will? Must you give me sour looks, because I am generous?"

"This," the Master said clearly, "is an image of the kingdom of heaven." It is a kingdom ruled by a Father who loves his children and, whenever he chooses, can love them outrageously. The preference love shows does not imply injustice at all; God simply cannot be constrained. His fatherly love is of the kind that knows no bounds.

In a way this parable is unnecessary; God does not need to tell us this. Jesus, however, wishes to tell us of his Father's wonders, of the extent of his love for the least and the last. The apostles will observe this economy in operation, even on earth as it is in heaven. And again the striking point is made that God is sovereign, that grace is bestowed outside the call of justice. No merely dutiful Father this—this is a loving Father, and love, when divine, is of a grander democracy than ours.

Even farther than this, God's anxious care extends beyond the last, even to the lost. This is absolutely shocking to Pharisees of whatever era. Seeing Jesus so often in the company of sinners and tax-collectors, some Pharisees archly delivered what they must have thought was a completely damning accusation: "Here is a man that entertains sinners, and eats with them!" True son of his Father in heaven, Jesus must have felt complimented.

What are the feelings, the Master asks, of the shepherd who, having left the ninety-nine good sheep untended, finally discovers the wayward one? Why, he is full of rejoicing. He calls together his friends and neighbors for a celebration. "So it is, I tell you, in heaven," Jesus informs them; "there will be more rejoicing over one sinner who repents than over ninety-nine souls that are justified." His Father is a father who will search for his lost children as zealously as that housewife who had lost a coin worth one-tenth of all she had. The real scandal is the unmitigated joy this unleashes. A stern and begrudged reproof would be all most fathers could muster.

God's Son has given us a deep look into his Father's mercy, an insight he will later amplify with the parable of the prodigal son. A strange court this will form for his kingly Father, such a flock of favored, repentant sinners! Yet to refuse to try to understand is to want God in our own image. The Lord knows better; he comes from this Father's house. These are lessons he has learned from him, and perhaps from his mother as well. (Could it have been a neighborhood party Jesus remembered Mary having after she had found a lost coin?) One learns to care, and how much to care, from parents.

These then are the scenes our Lord brings before us to make vivid the immense goodness of his Father. No, there is perhaps one more glimpse we get of what the Father is like when we see his Son tirelessly blessing the children brought to him. The disciples have decided that Jesus' patience is really excessive and have tried to steer the children away from the Master. The Lord is indignant because, as he points out, "the kingdom of God belongs to such as these." This was the work his Father wished; and too few adults permit him to love them. These children approach him properly, simply, with open arms. "And so he embraced them, laid his hands upon them, and blessed them."

The contemplation of Christ as the man of sorrows, if it is

too exclusive, can become a positive heresy. Forgotten, then, would be the fact that the element of joy in the Master's human life was immensely preponderant. That Jesus enjoyed the beatific vision of his Father surely is the basis of his joy. Just the same there are moments in his life when our Lord is more than usually happy in an earthly human sense. Right here, before the shadows of the Passion begin to engulf us, let us enjoy such a moment.

Jesus is engaged on the happiest of tasks: talking about his Father, telling us of his magnificence. Could there be any other subject he would prefer? He has come to bring his Father's blessing to the world. What a joy, now, to announce the outrageous extent to which his Father cares for each of us, even if we are last or lost or least! His holiness and generosity are beyond our imagining.

There is, however, a grave side to this relationship. Man must respond to God's love, and respond properly. Children, just because they are children, do not automatically become good children. For this reason the Master couples with his revelation of his Father's providence a series of lessons for us that underline the various characteristics that would make up the response of a dutiful and devoted son of God the Father.

First of all, it must never be forgotten that he is an almighty and divine Father. The familiarity to which we are invited, indeed drawn to, must not lead us to any brash lack of respect. However much we may be elated by such honor, it should not let slip our clear and humble sense of adoration before God's greatness. Two parables concerning great banquets are related to illustrate this.

In the first story the Master points out the embarrassment of a guest who over-rates himself and chooses the seat of honor at the feast. Humility should have, instead, made him well aware that the host could easily have invited some guest whose rank was greater. Furthermore, the disposition of honors belongs to the host alone. All this is overlooked in a rush of childish self-assertion and, beyond his station, this unfortunate fellow finds himself (as our Lord puts it), "taking, with a blush, the lowest place of all." The Master points out the only safe rule to be followed: choose the lowest place, for "everyone who exalts himself shall be humbled, and he that humbles himself shall be exalted." Plainly it is the Father who does the exalting, not ourselves.

The last are first again when the first invited to the Lord's supper beg off with excuses. Perhaps there have been too many of these great suppers, and this familiarity faults them into preferring something else in its place. But the host is enraged; his honor is offended; wives, farms, even oxen, have been put ahead of him. Is this not an easy scene to imagine? And we can let diminish in ourselves that lively recollection of God's greatness so easily. With so many "understandable" excuses we begin to prefer so many smaller matters to attending upon him.

What is at question here is a feeling of self-importance; it is our affairs that are of over-riding necessity. Lost in the swirl of details involving only ourselves is any memory of our prime duty to God the Father: adoration. In this life there can come the moment when some other duty can supersede honoring our earthly fathers. Not so with our Father in heaven. Only a foolish failure in humility could lead us to think ourselves any more than his needy children. We are dependent on him.

Nine of the ten lepers that Jesus cured forgot this. The Master was not right there beside them when the authorities certified their cleansing, freeing them from their exile from friends and family. Expressing their gratitude was simply not the most important thing they had to do with their first moments of freedom. God could come later. Except for the foreigner, who returned "praising God aloud," the lepers celebrated their independence elsewhere. Their physical independence had gone to their heads.

A true son of God has constant reason for gratitude to his Father in heaven, and his remembrance of his dependence must be constant. This is a second major characteristic of divine sonship.

How vividly aware of this the apostles must have been while the Master somberly reported the agonies in which this world will end. Who could listen without fear of this world's finish, unless assured that Christ himself would be there to help his faithful? Before forces of destruction such as these we know how helpless and dependent we truly are. In such straits our plea for help, for redress, comes quickly. The Master's exhortation to public prayer to the Father gets a good hearing at such a moment. It is also apparent that God "will give redress with all speed" to his children who "are crying out to him, day and night." "But, worries our Lord, with trepidation for us, "when the Son of Man comes, will he find faith left on the earth?" Just an occasional sense of dependence on God will not withstand much strain. Only a solid and uninterrupted habit of recognizing our total dependence on God's fatherly help will keep our hopes, amidst such pressures, centered on the only One who truly cares.

This is a day-by-day affair. To sink home how prone we all are to ridiculous little displays of self-confidence, the Master lets us watch as God watches two of his sons come to pray in his temple. One of them, a Pharisee, righteously stands before God and prays, "I thank you, God, that I am not like the rest of men. . . ." He goes on, but he has already revealed himself. He is no sinner, as he sees himself.

The tax-collector is not so brazen, says Jesus. "He would not even lift up his eyes towards heaven; he only beat his breast, and said, 'God, be merciful to me; I am a sinner.'" Having drawn so striking a contrast, the Master hardly has to tell us which one will be exalted and which humbled. A false piety makes the Pharisee's prayer reek, while it is the lowly Publican who, looking nowhere but to his Father, speaks the language of a son.

The Pharisee thinks he is rich; the Publican knows he is poor. The Pharisee thinks he is superior; the Publican knows better about himself. The Pharisee is talking to himself: the Publican is talking to his Father. Knowing his indigence, he pretends no independence, he asks only for mercy.

This Parisee is no straw-man that the Lord has set up. He is very real in every one of us. We all itch for pretended self-sufficiency. We all seem to have an urge to serve more than one master or make as if we serve none. Perhaps we are seeking outside aid that we can face more comfortably than God. It is all the same whether we try to console ourselves with faked riches within ourselves or material riches without. Both add up to the same foolish quest to be someone other than one of the Father's sons and subject to him.

It is precisely because this is such a tempting evasion and one so instinctive to our nature that Jesus speaks so vehemently about riches. To put it baldly, they are an enemy. They can block completely our relationship with our Father. "Where your treasure-house is, there your heart is too," our Lord warned his listeners at the end of his discourse on providence, knowing well our instinct is to bank on the things of this world.

The Master outlines the final outcome of the misuse of money and other material wealth with the vigorous portraits of two contemporaries, a certain rich man and Lazarus, a beggar who haunted his doorstep. The rich man lacked nothing here and everything hereafter while it was the humbled Lazarus who was exalted. Would it not seem that all those whom God had blessed with much on earth would have been the more faithful? Perhaps so, but this is not mankind's usual experience. Material blessings have, it seems, the power to render man insensate to God's direction. The only remedy is a rigorous internal sense of detachment. Most certainly we cannot avoid dealing with all these things—our very life is surrounded with physical needs—but they must never be allowed to assume more than their own modest significance. For a child of this earth things may look differently, but to the eyes of one of God's sons they should ever present but a pale and flimsy spectacle. God the Father provides; do not fret. With the transparency of a child who trusts his Father's provisions, we must develop a holy disregard for earthly possessions. Only then will we begin to be safe from this danger, this infection that riches carry. And it needs to be stressed that this is just to begin, for this is a battle that is only being won when we are still battling.

A new figure appears on the scene with a basic question for the Master: "What must I do to achieve eternal life?" This rich young man is a gentle and good fellow who, when quizzed by the Lord on the commandments, can honestly state that all of them he had kept always. "Where is it that I am still wanting?" he bravely asks. With a penetrating glance Jesus evaluates his statement and loves him for its truthfulness and his untapped potential. "In one thing you are still wanting," he begins.

"If you have a mind to be perfect, go home and sell all that belongs to you; give it to the poor, and so the treasure you have shall be in heaven; then come back and follow me." At the great invitation the poor fellow's face falls. He stops short where the child would rush on; he shies away from the full embrace of Christ and Christ alone. This blessing is too expensive. Lacking courage he recoils and goes away sorrowing, for great were his possessions.

Quickly Jesus turns to the twelve to drive home the lesson before them, saying, "With what difficulty will those who have riches enter God's kingdom!" Riches are a horrible drag on perfection. To immunize the rich against this virus requires, the Master asserts, a miracle of grace possible to God alone. The danger is that great. On the face of it, conceivably, anyone can be poor in spirit, but it is far safer to be poor in fact.

Children can count on their father for support. "Make it your first care to find the kingdom of God, and his approval, and all these [other] things shall be yours without the asking!" "You have a Father in heaven who knows you need them all." Do we fail to believe our Lord when he tells us this? What he requires is that we abandon our lives to him and his Father. He wants us totally at his service, unfettered by anything else but devotion to him.

His followers must have the freedom poverty gives, the open-handed and happy generosity that only the detached can have, if they would follow him. They will see families alienated, friends become enemies, and each one will bear a cross like his own. With all this to face no one can drag along as well all the baggage of the rich. Only the freedom of the sons of God will do, so count the cost, and remember how humble are the exalted.

Another characteristic close to this is the selfless, unstinting sense of duty that the Father expects. It was to underscore this that Jesus thoroughly surprised his audience one day by praising the unscrupulous steward who connived so when he saw his job was lost. His tireless efforts would have been praiseworthy indeed if his purpose had been right. Such, however, is not rarely the case with things of this world. Do we not have a supernatural welfare to protect as assiduously? We "children of light," with faces upraised to our Father above, must seek him with even more intense singlemindedness. We can, as true sons, give no less to our Father than our complete service.

It does not befit sons to question the wisdom of their Father or querulously to badger him with queries about what reward goes with each little action. We are to serve him wholeheartedly simply because it is our place to do so, it is our duty. We are servants—of God, to be sure—but servants none the less. We must learn to plead no one's cause but the Lord's; to seek no one's pleasure but his. Any other position but self-effacement is out of line.

In a statement of great and blunt power Jesus reaffirms this essential attitude. "And you, . . . when you have done all that was commanded you, are to say, *'We are servants and worthless; it was our duty to do what we have done.'*" The Father is not bound in gratitude to us. It is the other way around.

Of course such compliance is necessary for the proper and ordered functioning of the kingdom. Our labor is only going to be more than worthless when it fits into the pattern of God's providence, and then it is he who provides, not we. But our obedience and our collaboration would be disillusioning, at best, if their sole basis were discipline in God's army. The true dignity of our dutiful service is rooted far more deeply within ourselves and God's plans. We are truly God's sons, and of such is a son's service compounded. We are doing merely what we owe to God as duty, yet it is because of a dignity conferred on us that is resplendent.

Still this is a dignity that we can smear with sin. And then it is the part of the son to be honest in his contrition. To give us an example of this Jesus chooses to relate the parable that probes deepest into this marvelous father-son relationship between God and ourselves. It is the tale of a young son who prodigally wastes his patrimony. Penniless and humiliated, the son comes to his senses. "I will rise and go to my father," he vows, "and say to him, 'Father, I have sinned against heaven and before you; I am not worthy, now, to be called your son; treat me as one of your hired servants.'" He has destroyed all rights to his past status; he has derogated his sonship. The Master has pictured his change of heart with graphic, perfect words.

But, suddenly, the parable seems to turn in his hand. It is the father who was watching while the son forgot. It is the father who runs to meet his son. The erring son does not even get to complete his prepared confession before the father smothers it with orders for the best robe, a ring, and a fatted calf for feasting. It is no longer the parable of the prodigal son but of the prodigal father. Indeed the father is as reckless in loving as was the son in spending. No mortal heart would have dared to invent this parable, for it reveals the very heart of the Father in heaven.

The other elder son, petulant at this display, stigmatizes our human inability to forget ourselves. His bitter self-interest is so really horrible in contrast with his father's love. He has failed, however dutifully, to understand at all the father's sadness at his brother's loss. How could he? He had never abandoned himself to anything. Yet, all the same, the dead has come to life again. Rejoice, the lost is found.

GRADUALLY, THROUGHOUT THESE MONTHS OF WAITING FOR THE RIGHT MOMENT IN JERUSALEM, THE APOSTLES MUST HAVE COME TO AN AWED AWARENESS OF THE GREAT PERSONAL DEVOTION TO BE REQUIRED OF THEM. That they were inadequate was just as clear. Still, had they not simultaneously been treated to a vision of the Father's providential care that would offset their trembling?

They knew better how sons of God should respond to their Father's care: with humility, with an unvarnished sense of dependence, ever grateful, poor, obedient, respectful and devoted to service. These lessons unite to form the image of true piety, the virtue of filial service and affection. No simpering attitude this, it is a stance for action. No little sweet chain of pieties these, this is a position of service before our Father which will call from us every strength we have. So crucial, in fact, is this that the Holy Spirit will bring his gift as well to help us to harmonize in due measure piety's many sides. Indeed, as it is so transparently the ambition of Jesus so must it be ours: to be perfect sons to our outrageously provident Father in heaven.

The bridge between these placid days and the violence to follow is Bethany, suburb to Jerusalem. The end begins there most definitely as the Master defies death and raises Lazarus, his friend. The scene and the event are beyond description and beyond analysis. Jesus is so completely man in all he does, so completely God in his accomplishment.

Yet the resurrection of Lazarus is truly a conclusion to all the Master has taught these months. Jesus himself is the ministrant of the prodigal Father's care. Providence is enacted. Lazarus comes forth because he is God's son and a true one.

Jesus has proven his promise that "You have a Father in heaven who knows. . . ." And we, with the apostles, with Mary and Martha and Lazarus, must learn to answer with true piety and contrition: "We are servants and worthless; it was our duty to do what we have done." For it is a basic law of the kingdom that "Everyone who exalts himself shall be humbled; and he that humbles himself shall be exalted."

9 ZEAL

The Last Week

A LIVE LAZARUS IS MORE THAN THE PHARISEES CAN STAND. In council to meet this crisis they talk out their anxiety. Jesus is their problem. "If we leave him to his own devices," they complain, "he will find credit everywhere. Then the Romans will come and make an end of our city and our race."

The motives for their panic stand revealed. They fear loss of their privileged position and fear, too, that by removing them the Romans may complete the political subjection of their people. The enormity of Lazarus' resurrection demands action, but they are at a loss as to what to do.

The cutting voice of a collaborator stills the confusion. Caiaphas speaks: "You have no perception at all; you do not reflect that it is best for us if one man is put to death for the sake of the people, to save a whole nation from destruction." Jesus is to be their scapegoat. The resolution of death is passed; the plot is laid.

In this rare glimpse into the Jewish council we are treated to a scene of frightened decision. Hardly more than a week will pass before the bile and cunning of Caiaphas find full scope. Yet have we heard any voice that would indicate that these were religious leaders? Instead their resolutions are bared as selfish. Religiosity will decorate them later for public consumption. For all its ardor their zeal remains a false zeal, an exalted and intense self-concern. Sadly, however, it does not by that fact lose its power. Zeal, so fiercely powerful, can wreak wonders or horrors.

The gospels tell us frankly that the apostles were "bewildered" and "faint-hearted." We can see that they were badly shaken. The extent of the animosity Jesus had caused among the rulers was frightening. Rather than falsely reassure the apostles, the Master truly reassures them, foretelling again in precise detail what is to happen: passion, death and, finally, victorious resurrection. But what he says is lost on them. "They could make nothing of all this." Perhaps it is merciful that they do not, for they have not the heart to face what is coming.

Two of them, at least, are not paralyzed with fear. James and John, with their mother Zebedee in the lead, approach the Lord with a brash request. Their mother would have Jesus promise her boys the places at his right and left when he achieves his glory.

It is somewhat surprising to see the Master not rebuke this display of ambition. Instead he gently inquires: "Have you strength to drink of the cup I am to drink?" They answer firmly, "We have," little knowing how greatly they have committed themselves. But the Master has seen the generosity in their hearts. Their unformed zeal has taken this ambiguous and awkward way to express itself. Indeed, they do not know what it is they ask. On that account alone, though, Jesus does not reprove them. He would bring this zeal to perfection.

Not so deeply understanding is the reaction of the other

apostles who have witnessed this little scene. The human resentment of anything that resembles crass self-promotion set them burning with jealous indignation. Before the bickering can even begin Jesus calls them about him. Now he strikes deep with his rebuke. Each one was hanging his head.

You are not to be like the worldly powerful, he begins; "Whoever would be a great man among you, must be your servant, and whoever has a mind to be first among you, must be everybody's slave." If you all must jostle for places around me, the wisest choice is the lowliest, Jesus tells them. They have heard this before.

One might wonder at Christ's reaction to such pettiness at the crucial stage of his career. Yet there is no hint of irritation in his words as he goes on to expose to them the depths of meaning within this attitude. Despite its immensely stirring overtones, his next statement probably does little more for the twelve than deepen their embarrassment. "So it is that the Son of Man did not come to have service done him," Jesus proclaims, "he came to serve others, and to give his life as a ransom for the lives of many." Such is the selfless zeal the Lord spends on us. No apostle of whatever age can have any other model for the zeal he must strive to purify within himself. No less a zeal will enable him, like his Master, "to give his life as a ransom for many." Any less pure a sense of dedication makes us liable to the distorted zeal of the Pharisees.

Crowds are now streaming after Jesus as he circles round towards Jerusalem. At first sight it seems to be a crowd full of genuine admiration for the Master. Yet it is a tense group— were not the days becoming ever more tense?—and one easily irritated. A blind man, crying out for the Lord's attention, is told to be quiet. He may be bothering the onlookers but not the Master, and Jesus cures blind Bartimaeus. Persistent faith is the seedbed for divine action. Zeal can grow only from such roots.

More crowds of the curious await him in Jericho. So great is the press of people around him that prosperous Jericho's tax-collector, rich Zacchaeus, has to climb a tree to gain sight of Jesus. Unscrupulous people are often quite unscrupulously honest with themselves and quite without foolish pride. His spry effort does not go unnoticed. "Make haste and come down," says the Master to Zacchaeus, perched up there. And as the Lord goes off to eat with him, the crowd shows that it, too, can be pharisaical. They are indignant, for "he has gone," they complain, "to lodge with one who is a sinner." Ironically, this balances the shock of the rich over the Master consorting with the poor. Jesus, however, is the out-and-out partisan only of his Father; no social class has exclusive rights on him. With a bit of the Pharisee in each of them, the crowd fails to adjust to this event and petulantly reveals its shallowness. That Zacchaeus publicly promises a tax-refund for all as well as great largesse to the poor seems to have thoroughly eased the situation.

It is clear that the crowd is not leading Jesus. They cannot limit within their limitations the zeal of Christ. "That is what the Son of Man has come for," the Master patiently explains once more, "to search out and to save what was lost." And clearly no prejudice can put boundaries on this search. A zeal no less than universal can satisfy Christ or Christians.

To calm the impatient messianic expectations of triumph building fiercely about him, Jesus relates a parable of personal responsibility, a parable with waiting in it. Leaving his servants with various amounts of money to work with while he is away, a certain nobleman leaves only to return as their king.

Jesus is, of course, the king who, on his return, asks for an accounting. Every man, born as a servant of the sovereign master, is bound to make the goods received by him bear fruit. Neglect or forgetfulness or timidity all are but types of dereliction of duty. The reward is not simply measured by results, since abilities differ, but by the zeal employed, by the labor expended. This is true "richness": to be ever employing to their utmost the talents God has given. They are not to be cherished privately in some safety-deposit box. Zeal is not zeal at all if it is not always searching for accomplishment in God's name, in this king's name.

The last stop-over on the road to Jerusalem is the friendly oasis of Bethany. There a whole flock of his friends have prepared a feast for him. It should have been a warm and relaxed evening, but the tension about them all was too much to be quieted. It is Mary Magdalen who intuits the gravity of the moment. Through the din and clamor of history blasting towards its climax it seems that only she has heard and heeded the Master's grave words of prophecy about his death.

As a somber act of farewell Mary pours on the head and feet of Jesus a jar of precious spikenard. The ointment was worth at least a year's pay and everyone there gasped at the extravagance. For the first time Judas becomes spokesman for the group, complaining that such treasure should better have been given to the poor. It was certainly not the first time, nor the last, that the grasping would gasp at the profligacy of love and dress their outrage in insincere, pious words. The other disciples join Judas in this protest.

Sharply Jesus intervenes in Mary's defense. She sees further than all of you, he announces; this nard will, prophetically, serve for my burial; her act will be ever honored because she did it to me. Later, failing in opportunities to love me in person, you will then have to love me in the person of the poor.

But what has Mary done? Beyond the simple facts, there is one conclusion only: hers is an act of deeply disturbed, absolute and humble love. It is humble in its unabashed revelation of her past; she has dried her Lord's feet with her hair before. Deeply disturbed, she has foreboded her Master's death and offered ahead of time a sacrifice of her own. It is so absolute as to be oblivious of all else. She has, indeed, loved much! Zeal is love in full ardor, vehemently serving its object. And so incomprehensible must it ever be, unless we see the depth and force of the love beneath it. This scene, furthermore, should lead us to think twice before criticizing, from some commonplace stance, the extravagant act of love. That a deed be done with the touch of inspiration, that it seem impetuous or immoderate—these characteristics, however much they may unsettle us who love less, may well be the signs of true zeal. The zealous, after all, are in the grip of God. And so it is with the Magdalen; she has seen far beyond the false climax the next day will bring.

AS THE GREAT PASSOVER APPROACHES, THE VALLEY OF THE CEDRON, WHICH HOLLOWS OUT THE SPACE BETWEEN MOUNT OLIVET AND THE HOLY CITY, BECAME A VAST ENCAMPMENT FOR THOUSANDS OF PILGRIMS. From all over Israel, many are eager to see Jesus. When the word is passed that the Master is on his way from Bethany a crowd swarms up and over Olivet towards him.

Jesus has made a decision; he will come to Jerusalem riding on an ass; prophecy ordains it so. The apostles only realize that the Master is permitting some sort of demonstration, and this breaks the dike holding everyone's pent-up enthusiasm. Now he will claim their honor and his messianic titles. The hour comes when, with no evasion, he will state: "Yes, I am a king." Garments are spread to saddle the animal ceremoniously. More are laid in its path. Palms and tree-branches are strewn along the way. Suddenly we are swept into triumphal procession. Hosannas ring out.

Olivet's peak reached, the crowd becomes a tribe, an army surrounding the king of peace, king of Salem. The whole mass is infected with unbridled acclamation: hosanna! The Pharisees, knowing Christ's past reticence, demand that he quiet this sedition, but it is beyond arresting. It is a spontaneous surge of ovation. The cloaking of his kingship could only be temporary. "Son of David, king of Israel, hosanna!" Quiet these, the Master remarks to the Pharisees, and the stones beneath your feet would keep up the cry! We are in the midst of the one moment in Christ's life when he is acclaimed as his dignity deserves.

Reaching the height of the mount, one gasps at the view from Olivet's head. Gleaming like a jewel across the valley lies Jerusalem the beautiful and beloved. Instinctively the procession falters, distracted and reverent for a moment before this vision of the holy city. Through the din of triumph failure forebodes. Of a sudden two levels of the Lord's consciousness become manifest together. He sees all with a sort of x-ray vision; this city's whole history streams before him all at once. In the middle of this triumphal moment he weeps. Jesus weeps because he loves Jerusalem and knows that, despite this moment's noise, his coming would go unheeded and unwelcomed. This magnificent city he sees as destroyed and desolate, "all because you did not recognize the time of my visiting you." How temporary is the glory of this world!

After this pause, this moment of truth, the mood of joy sweeps over the scene again. The procession loudly continues down and over to Jerusalem across its avenue of palms, pageantry and the glad shouts of children. His coming is eagerly awaited within the city by the ever-present blind and lame. He cures them. The enthusiastic shouts ring out still louder. There in the temple, some Greeks approach like foreign correspondents. Finally all is hushed to hear the words of this conquering king.

"The time is come now," Jesus begins, "for the Son of Man to achieve his glory." Yet how startled must that crowd have been as he went on to detail how this paschal mystery would be celebrated: life from death, death to life itself! He, their king of kings, is the seed falling from the hand of the Father to die so that it can bloom. Mysterious eternal paradox: lose to gain, die to live! It will be true, too, of all who truly follow him.

The human hardship in accomplishing this looms before Christ's mind; he is distressed, fearful, upset. Quickly he submits his human will to the divine: "Father," he cries out in anguish, "make your name known!" He fully commits himself to his Father's plans.

And the Father speaks. As at the beginning of his public life and at the transfiguration, so now at the beginning of his sacrifice the Father accredits his Son. And the Son turns to tell the stunned crowd that the moment of crisis is upon them. "Sentence is now being passed on this world; now is the time when the prince of this world is to be cast out. Yes, if only I am lifted up from the earth, I will attract all men to myself!" The king that they honor is to rule from a cross. He is a sacrificial king bringing life beyond this world and beyond death. He will be no other sort of king.

And so Palm Sunday ends in shadows, a triumph that truth has sobered, and soon would slaughter. The Lamb of God has been dressed for sacrifice.

WHAT AN IMMENSE AND STRANGE SPECTACLE THIS DAY HAS SEEN!
How are we to understand it, knowing what is to happen
within the week? The key is, of course, the crowd, so full now
of hosannas. Theirs is but a surface loyalty to Jesus, compounded of genuine admiration, national frustration and false
worldly messianic hopes. Not having accepted the years of
preparation Christ has spent on them, it is already too late for
depth and perception. Pride and religious superficiality are not
overcome by mob action; they are, instead, increased. Way
beyond their depth, their commitment to the Lord is slight and
fickle, no matter how loud their praise.

What is to be said of its zealous and enthusiastic acclaim?
Simply that it is not enough. Precisely here emerges the reason
behind the failure of Jerusalem and its people: the only zeal
they show, or have shown, for God's house and God's plans has
been shallow, selfish and short-lived. God is not truly served by
short-winded words or works empty and momentary. True zeal
is not so superficial; it is deep and interior and rooted in a full
commitment to God's will.

Real zeal honestly faces the extent of its commitment. No
number of hosannas could hide from Jesus the frightening
vision of where zeal would take him. He honestly cringes
before such a spending of himself; no slight enthusiasm will
carry him through such trial. He states the problem with fear-
less clarity: "Believe me when I tell you this; a grain of wheat
must fall into the ground and die, or else it remains nothing
more than a grain of wheat; but if it dies, then it yields rich
fruit. He who loves his life will lose it. . . . " And so that we
may not think this is not our problem, too, the Master adds,
"If anyone is to be my servant, he must follow my way"—this
way of total commitment.

Zeal, so completely removed from any simple frenzy of

good works, must be very deeply rooted. It is into these depths of dedication that the Master is now entering. The pressures are becoming so strong that the Lord's acts now take on the absolute temper of his most profound energies.

Leaving Bethany early the next morning, probably without breakfast, Jesus is hungry. There is a fig tree beside the road and the Master seeks, out of season, to pick its fruit. It is barren, of course, but Jesus curses it and it withers into nothing. How unlike Christ, one first reacts! Is this not a cruel gesture, to strike this fig tree? It is cruelly symbolic, the harsh truth most harshly exemplified. The hour has come; Israel must bear fruit or be struck for its barrenness. This striking act is in the tradition of the prophets, and it becomes a stark overture to the deeds and discourses of this day and the next.

This same absolute mood remains as the Master enters the temple. Once before he drove from his Father's house all the clutter of business and money-changing. This morning he will cleanse the temple for the last time. With a whip of cords, the Lord charges violently upon the offenders—sheep, oxen and pigeons take flight before him. Their masters flee in fright; their attacker, they can see, is a man possessed. The coins of the money-changers roll every which way as their owners desert them. To their cowering, retreating figures the Master, terrible in rage, hurls his charge: "My house shall be known for a house of prayer, and you have made it into a den of thieves!"

Such vehemence! No wonder that the disciples would remember that saying from the psalms, "Zeal for your house will consume me!" The chief priests and Pharisees are struck dumb. However speechless now, their false zeal must have been burning within them. Clearly the Master was no one to be argued with this day.

Nor was he the next. To their prompt attack, asking,

What is the authority by which you do these things?" Jesus coolly counter-attacks with a question of his own. When they falter, he regally states his conclusion: "The publicans and harlots are further on the road to God's kingdom than you!" This is followed by two parables so fiercely explicit that they must have made their hearers shudder.

The unfaithful vinedressers who plot to murder the owner's son, who can they be but his hearers? The very voice of Caiaphas is heard in the parable as they decide to murder. "And now," the Master concludes, "what will the owner of the vineyard do to those vinedressers when he returns? He will bring those wretches to a wretched end." The violence of it wrenches from the crowd a fervent "God forbid," but they continue to forbid him.

To complete his indictment of Israel's infidelity Jesus chooses to repeat an image he has used before, that of the banquet that the invited guests spurn. This time, however, he stiffens the parable with dire details. Those who refuse the invitation now are destroyed and their cities leveled. The razing of Jerusalem is still on our Lord's mind. Furthermore, gaining entrance to the banquet is not enough. Complete and continuing acceptance must be given to this invitation. To be discovered without a wedding garment is to be "cast into the darkness, where there shall be weeping, and gnashing of teeth." The tragic plight of Israel is unmistakable.

The Pharisees are not cowed. They return with a captious question calculated to force the Master into preferring "Church or State." Much more are you the "collaborators" Jesus retorts, before he disposes of their problem with deceptive simplicity: "Give back to Caesar what is Caesar's, and to God what is God's." The Sadducees try their hand at confounding him and they, too, end up discountenanced. Another try, more feeble yet, is made and ends no better. Their vaunted superiority has been destroyed. They have been thoroughly mastered, and to their defeat Jesus appends a crushing condemnation.

Never has any party been as ruthlessly shamed, and as rightly. With seven maledictions Jesus unfolds before his hearers the hypocritical wickedness of these men. They are unmerciful, ostentatious, proud and greedy despoilers. One by one he lays bare the ugliness of their spiritual pretenses. His scathing denunciation becomes most horrible in conclusion: "It was your fathers who slaughtered the prophets; it is for you to complete your fathers' reckoning. Serpents that you are, brood of vipers, how should you escape from the award of hell?" They are not descendants of the prophets, but offspring of their murderers and undertakers, and they will not fail to climax this murderous tradition.

Is Jesus bitter? No, it is more a matter of deep sorrow; bitterness would lead Christ to dismiss his nation as worthless, not beloved. He closes this terrible discourse with a lament of agonizing tenderness: "Jerusalem, Jerusalem, still murdering the prophets, and stoning the messengers that are sent to you, how often have I been ready to gather your children together, as a hen gathers her chickens under her wings; and you refuse it!" Only this warmth tempers his indictment of their infidelity. Yet the end of love spurned is irretrievable: an empty heritage, desolate and barren. "Behold, your house is left to you, a house uninhabited." And with this frightening and sad menace, he stops.

Never again does he speak to the people he so loves.

Zeal, clearly, has its antipathies. Sin and infidelity, if they persist, cannot abide with God. The hour has come when this world is to be judged. And zeal has made Jesus into the instrument of divine decree. Zeal for his Father's house has brought us this Jesus, an implacable destroyer of resistance to his Father. Knowing no compromise with unrepentant evil, our Lord is measuring his world as God's justice measures it.

The Master is now drawn up to prophetic stature. He seems entirely preoccupied with Israel's whole destiny. Utterly abstract, he is seeing with eternity's finality, and with that view's absolute division of sheep and goats. Coldly he pronounces Israel dead, describes her pharisaical undertakers, details her burial. This view has its beauties: new guests will still more fully pack the kingdom. Yet, the Lord's whole being has been elevated and absorbed to an extent unique in his life. Here Jesus is least human, drawn into the upper reaches of himself. Indeed, the most harrowing note in the judgment of the Pharisees is its crystal frigidity. This chilling menace of Israel's ruin and destruction is only kept Christian by the love exposed in the "how often I have been ready to gather your children together. . . ."

It is with relief that we watch the Master rest for a moment. He is tired after this intense struggle. A poor widow comes up to the treasury of the temple and throws in her two mites. Showing his inner composure and perception, the Master notes the magnificent gesture of the widow, for she had "put in all she had." How this lightens the terrible depression brought on by all that has been said! There is yet light and goodness and true religion in the world, however insignificantly exposed. Zeal, even removed and exalted, can never be blind to goodness.

THIS DAY IS NOT ENDED. As the tiny band, the twelve and their leader, pass out of the holy city, how can they fail to be moved by what has happened? Out the city gates they pass, through gates that seem indestructible. When would this enormous downfall, this negative sacrament, occur? They ask Jesus.

They unleash a tidal wave of grave prophecy. One horrendous detail after another is spilled out. The Master is feeling ultimate and is expressing himself from so high above man's view of providence that it is not hard to imagine how difficult it was for the apostles to disentangle these distresses. All at once before our Lord's eyes come, in compenetrating layers, the destruction of his beloved Jerusalem and the final end of the world. This dreadful and prolonged description comes to one conclusion: be ever ready, ever watchful.

Their zeal must never flag. "What I say to you," Jesus warns, "I say to all, watch!" The hour of the end, the very moment of it, no one will suspect; "it will come like the springing of a trap." The only resolution to face these horrors with is constant preparedness. But zeal must have its plan, its shape. And this the Master reveals inasmuch as the apostles must know it.

These directions are enshrined in two parables, that of the ten virgins and the talents, plus a description of how the final judgment will be conducted. The pivotal point of the parable of the ten virgins is the delay—all fall asleep while waiting for the bridegroom to arrive. The five foolish virgins suddenly find themselves unprepared, and left out.

Clear as this is, the parable of the talents provides the twelve with instructions on what they are to do while the Master "is long in coming." The tale of the ten virgins could have led them to think their task was merely one of maintenance and preservation. No, the task of the Church is to be progressive and expansive. Jesus is not just leaving so as to surprise us on returning. We are to work and to achieve in his absence, multiplying his legacy. Faithful over little things, the "joy of the Lord" will be ours. And this fidelity to little things—which must have meant for Jesus his little ones—foreshadows his next and final pronouncement before the end.

The king sits in judgment on all mankind assembled. And what is the scrutiny he makes? It is on man's zealous love for his neighbor because of Christ's identity with the poor. Thus charity is described as the only essential attitude; rather, its position at the peak is to indicate that, however necessary other activities are, they are worthless unless imbued with charity. At this point this is not entirely clear to the apostles; Thursday's teaching will complete it. The role of zeal is clear, nonetheless. It must reach for every opportunity. We can dare to miss no one lest we fall victim to that terrible sentence: "When you refused it to one of the least of my brethren here, you refused it to me."

And what is the motive for this? It is to carry out God's plans, to glorify Jesus, and through him the Father. We must be as full of zeal as we are full of love for our Master. It is him we shall zealously serve in the last, the lost and the least. It is his stature we must imitate, trying ever to see things from his height and with his clarity, ever seeking to reproduce in ourselves that most disturbing characteristic of his, his eminent spiritual energy. No man has ever lived as he lived. Yet, with intense ardor, we must generously commit ourselves to following him completely. All else, obviously, is chaos.

One last episode completes this week of shock and triumph. Judas, one of the twelve, rescues the Pharisees from witless defeat. For thirty pieces of silver he proposes to sell them Jesus. Before the Pharisees Judas is a sick man; the kiss in the garden will show his final value, one utterly lost to goodness. This sad bargain is sealed, and sealed too is the fate of Israel. All that is left is to work out the tragic details.

"The Son of Man did not come to have service done him; he came to serve others, and to give his life as a ransom for others." To be truly his followers must we not say as well, "Zeal for your house will consume me"?

10 CHARITY

The Last Day

THE TWENTY-FOUR HOURS OF HISTORY, THAT THROUGH HORROR
BRING PEACE TO THE WORLD, BEGIN IN PEACE. Intimacy, solemn
and immense, pervades the upstairs room to which Jesus and
his twelve retire to celebrate the paschal meal. The stern pres-
sure of crisis is upon them too; climax insists its moment has
come.

"Jesus already knew," the gospel informs us, "that the time
had come for his passage from this world to the Father. He still
loved those who were his own, whom he was leaving in the
world, and he would give them the uttermost proof of his love."
A climactic exhibition of masterful love, this is this day's goal.
Jesus would leave this legacy most vivid: his divine-human love
so explained and enacted before them as to be an unforgettable
example for them to follow and fulfill.

Mankind's salvation and sanctification are to be, princi-
pally, this day's doing. The Master will leave behind all history's preparations to bring the final, true Passover into being.
He has come among us to announce and accomplish God's love

for men. So we can thrill to the fervor that vibrates in the opening words of Jesus at this supreme pasch: "I have longed and longed to share this paschal meal with you. . . ."

An all too familiar scuffle occurs before the meal even gets underway. Again the apostles are being petty and fractious over which among them is to have the more honored place. It is quite an index of how apparently slight an effect Christ's previous corrections have had. Words have not been enough to sink home even this lesson. And the Master plans to go so far beyond. He hopes to unfold the chief lesson of love, of Christian charity. It is a disheartening moment for him.

Silently he slips off his cloak, dons a towel and, before the twelve hardly realize what he is about, begins to wash their feet. Of a sudden all their contentions were stilled by shock. We can imagine the apostles mulling over this mute rebuke, feeling their shame increase as Jesus passes among them, kneeling and washing foot after foot. Peter breaks the silence, blurting out that it is all wrong, the Lord washing feet. With vehement humility he refuses to let Jesus wash him. Peter seems frightened at the thought. But what if that means you and I are no longer friends? the Master asks. A higher fear of any separation from Jesus forces Peter to the other extreme: wash every bit of me! It appears unlikely that anyone else would challenge the Lord. In stunned quiet the God-man finished his task and redressed himself for the banquet.

"Do you understand," he begins, "what it is I have done to you? You hail me as the Master and the Lord; and you are right, it is what I am. Why then, if I have washed your feet, I who am the Master and the Lord, you in your turn ought to wash each other's feet." Greatness and humility are partners in Christ and among Christians. In serving others nothing is beneath the Lord; he will slave for them; and no apostle is greater than his sender. The Master sums up: "I have been setting you an example, which will teach you in your turn to do what I have done for you; . . . blessed are you if you perform it!"

Jesus has not bidden us to have pity on men to whom we consider ourselves superior. He has bidden us to love them like brothers; indeed, to choose even a lower place. We are to love every man as though he were above us, not beneath us. We are to count it an honor to kneel before him and slave for him. How out of place is any disdain, any movement of self-dramatization!

If anything will engrave this lesson in our hearts let it be the sight of Jesus, genuflected, washing the feet of Judas. He is giving an "uttermost proof of his love."

It is to no avail. Frightened and fed up, Judas clinches his own internal bargain with Satan and Jesus, knowing this, announces to the twelve that one of them will betray him. Everyone has enough self-knowledge to wonder if it is himself; one need not wonder. Except for Peter and John, and Judas himself, the betrayer's secret is kept. The Master even covers the traitor's retreat with an ambiguous "Be quick on your errand." Judas flees in near panic.

The stakes of love are high; great glory or great guilt are its alternatives. Even now the Master has not retracted his love for Judas. He will not force his love on anyone, but nothing will force him to cease loving. The stakes are that high.

The formal Passover meal is all but over when the Master breaks from its ritual. "While they were still at table, Jesus took bread, and blessed, and broke it, and gave it to his disciples, saying, 'Take, eat, this is my body, given for you; do this for a commemoration of me.'" Taking a cup of wine he continued, "Drink, all of you, of this; for this is my blood, of the new testament, shed for many, to the remission of sins."

Penetrating awe settles over the table as Jesus speaks the

words of consecration; bread becomes his body, wine his blood. Separate but equal consecrations sunder, like a sword, his body and soul in sacrificial death. Really, though mystically, Calvary has occurred; redemption is here; the Lamb of God is slain and eaten!

Giving himself entirely to his Father, Jesus gives himself to his apostles. They evince no surprise; they have been promised this meal; indeed, they are empowered to re-do it for all of us. They eat his flesh and drink his blood. The Lord completely communicates himself; he is in them and they will live because of him, having his life within their own. Love has reached its term; by this astounding, literal gift of self, he is one with them. Divine love has given the "uttermost proof of his love." He has given everything: himself, body, blood, soul and divinity.

This early then has come the climax of the last supper. In symbol and in truth the Lord has done, ahead of time, his sacrifice, and shared love's conquest with his chosen. In triumph he cries out, "Now the Son of Man has achieved his glory, and in his glory God is exalted!"

From his personal achievement Jesus turns to point out to the apostles the new plateau of life to which they are lifted. Such holy communion with him means they must love with his love, loving each other and all others. The very breath of life at this height, "the mark by which all men will know you for my disciples," the Master proclaims, "will be the love you bear one another."

What follows this peak is Jesus speaking within the new unity, explaining what he has done, will do, and will have them do. And he must also say farewell, for this is his last supper.

Peter and the others are overcome with awareness of the new life they have, forgetting they bear it in vessels of clay.

So close to Jesus now, they worry over his comment on leaving them. This will be their mental preoccupation for most of the suppertime remaining. Boldly Peter protests that Jesus cannot leave him because he will go anywhere with him, even to death.

A frightening answer comes: "Tonight you will all lose courage over me!" The Master then attempts to forewarn his eleven of what is coming. Again they fail to attend to his words. Peter, even though promised that he will, after trial, return "to be the support of the brethren," bridles at the least hint of weakness on his part. His bluster draws from the Master the reluctant prophecy that Peter will thrice disown his Lord before morning. Still more protests from Peter and the rest are all the understanding Jesus receives. His further efforts to indicate how prepared they must be for a world gone mad and full of hatred evoke no deeper response than one apostle's light-headed, uncomprehending prattle, "See, Lord, here are two swords." To his bewildered band Jesus replies, with indulgent irony, "That is enough." They are not mature enough in their new love to realize how easily they may fail to live up to it.

"Do not let your heart be distressed; as you have faith in God, have faith in me." Sound advice this, to be remembered when he and they are all separated. Finishing his work, the Master will take his leave, to prepare a home for them in heaven. "And now," the Lord concludes cryptically, "you know the way to where I am going." Urgently Thomas protests that they know neither his destination nor his route; they are at sea.

"I," the Master proclaims, "am the way; I am truth and life; nobody can come to the Father, except through me." From this night on a way will be open to the Father's house; Jesus is that bridge-builder, that mediator. He is the truth showing the heaven-ward path and the life-giving force that propels movement towards the goal. All these are effects of that loving accomplishment the apostles now share in holy communion. Only through himself, the Master has revealed, only because of this new unity, can anyone join the Father in heaven. He is the only way. Henceforward every Christian prayer will end "through Christ our Lord. Amen."

Jesus is leaving and will return, but although he will still be with the apostles it will be in a different way. Between the ascension and the parousia comes the intermission of the Spirit. Another advocate is "called in" to care for the Church, the spirit of truth, as holy and divine as the Father and the Son. He will befriend them, defend them, and enlighten by guiding them "into all truth." The basic assurance the Lord is offering them on his departure is that there is to be no gap in God's concern for his Church. A change there will be, but it will not be a change in God's love. They are too close for that.

Indeed, "If a man has any love for me, he will be true to my word; and then," promises the Master, "he will win my Father's love, and we will both come to him, and make our continual abode with him." Practical love of Christ calls down the Father's love and brings about a joint visitation of Father and Son, not passing but abiding. The trinity will live, like friends, in our souls.

Such an unprecedented, undreamed of marvel! How will it be possible to bridge the infinite gap between divinity and us? Nothing other than a divine gift could confer divine friendship. And God does not stoop to our level; his friends are raised to his height. What is communicated to man is a share in God's life that becomes the foundation of this charity-friendship. There is created in man such a resemblance to God that he can be God's friend and God can live in him.

God Father, Son and Holy Spirit form no abstract, distant deity pouring itself out coldly in creating and preserving the world from afar. They form a real, living love internally intimate to God's sons.

This interior and absolute peace is a possession of the Lord's. No danger will or can mar the serenity such a communion with God gives. This, Jesus wants his chosen to share. "Peace," he tells them, "is my bequest to you, and the peace which I give you is mine to give; I do not give peace as the world gives it." Supernatural peace is beyond the powers of this world. Yet the powers of the world are to have their moment of apparent triumph soon. They will bring no worldly peace, but the Master will submit to their fury, he explains to the apostles, because "the world must be convinced that I love the Father." Peace is the product of that love, and none other.

This is not a passive union; it is always active and alive. Love is ever full of exchanges. It pulsates between parties, always in contact with one another, seeking every outlet, acting in concert. "I am the vine, you are its branches." Jesus reveals, "If a man lives on in me, and I in him, then he will yield abundant fruit; separated from me, you have no power to do anything." Separation kills; the branch does not give, it takes life from the vine. Jesus is the unique source; the life and love of Christian life and love can only be his. This vital immanence is the effect of God-living-in-them for the purpose of achieving God's glory. This is the prime goal of Christ and his Church, vine and branches.

"My Father's name has been glorified, if you yield abundant fruit, and prove yourselves my disciples," the Lord reminds them. There is to be discipline in this. "I have bestowed my love upon you, just as my Father has bestowed his love upon me; live on, then, in my love. You will live on in my love, if you keep my commandments, just as it is by keeping my Father's commandments that I live on in his love."

To conform to God's desires is to love with a disinterested

love, to stake all for the welfare of the beloved. How sad that so many Christians will miss this mark and flounder in the mediocrity of a love which seeks its own satisfaction first. Indeed, if there is no great love in our lives—pushing us out beyond ourselves—we are subhuman. We will have rendered sterile the love we could see transformed into God's love alive for all. In fact, by seeking our good in the Beloved, we grow, even to the heroic point of finding our happiness in self-sacrifice. This is the peak intensity of love, and it is at this summit that Jesus joyfully stands.

"All this I have told you," he confides, "so that my joy may be yours, and the measure of your joy may be filled up." How great the joy of being one with God, living and loving in his name.

Such love must find expression. And it is here that the Master reveals the full glory of our union with him. "This is my commandment, that you should love one another, *as I have loved you.*" This is a love far beyond that which God placed in the depths of our nature. We are commanded to love with God's love. With the love by which God loves himself, we are to love men as he loves them. Such is the transformation done in us that we will love with his love, be strong with his strength, do good with his goodness, be patient with his patience, because we are holy with his holiness.

There will be different vocations, different outlets for this divine love, yet the quality of this love must be ever the same. It is to be Christian. It is to know no limit.

"This is the greatest love a man can show," the Lord goes on, "that he should lay down his life for his friends; and you, if you do all I command you, are my friends." No corner of self reserved, the love towards which Jesus is leading us led him to his agony. Sacrifice becomes the test of friendship, and the friend who is loved to death is loved indeed. The Lord will not disguise this high challenge from them; they are now no longer servants, they are friends, and he loves them so.

Men in the world about us are no longer strangers. They are brothers. They are neighbors, part of ourselves. Sharing with them, really or potentially, the same divine life, we must desire their good as we desire our own. Vigorously we must love our neighbor as we love ourselves. This is the new commandment. "The task I have appointed you is to go out and bear fruit, fruit which will endure. . . . These are the directions I give you, that you should love one another."

No one is more aware than Jesus that this love is to be spent on a world that wants none of it. "If the world hates you," he harshly predicts, "be sure that it hated me before it learned to hate you. If you belonged to the world, the world would know you for its own and love you; it is because you do not belong to the world, because I have singled you out from the midst of the world, that the world hates you. They will persecute you just as they have persecuted me." Yes, love's stakes are high; love will cost all a man can pay. For himself and for his disciples the Lord has no illusions.

They must not be overwhelmed by the world's reaction, whether hate or, what is worse, indifference. "I have told you this," Jesus warns, "so that your faith may not be taken unawares." You must let no shock in this world shake you loose from your faith in God's love.

There are few people on earth, sad to say, who know how to love like Jesus, and hence, like the apostles, we run the risk of being lost in an unloving crowd. The Christian's love, furthermore, will often so contradict the world's inclinations that strife and persecution are to be hallmarks of Christ's Church.

The next twenty-four hours will bring enough of such horror to last for an eternity. That is not all; like its Master, Christ's Church will be in agony until time is done. There are, indeed, terrible shocks in store for the eleven and all who follow them in loving with divine love. Only being rooted in such an immense love will save them, and make their self-sacrifice a joy. They must place their confidence nowhere else.

"Believe me when I tell you this, you will weep and lament while the world rejoices; you will be distressed . . . but one day I will see you again, and then your hearts will be glad; and your gladness will be one which nobody can take away from you." This vista, however glorious in conclusion, leaves us in the harsh present. Carrying our crosses after Jesus will never be comfortable; it can never be. Yet it is as true that one cannot love without discomfort, without great suffering.

The great supper discourse is coming to a close. With alacrity the apostles express their wonder at their Master's words. "This gives us faith," they say, "that you were sent by God."

Back to his mind rush the thoughts of their flight and the agony that awaits him alone. "Yet I am not alone," Jesus assures himself, as we must always also do, "because the Father is with me." He turns, then, to sum up all he has said, seeking to assuage the grief they are soon to face. "I have said this to you, so that in me you may find peace. In the world, you will only find tribulation; but take courage, I have overcome the world."

As they rise to sing the closing psalms the last supper ends.

Passing down and out of the supper-room into the bright night light of the paschal moon, one last consolation awaits them. They are about to witness a most moving proof of their new elevation to familiarity with God. The Lord Jesus begins aloud to pray to his Father. It is his own Passover prayer.

"Father," he begins, "the time has come." The Lord's

prayer for himself asks for his own return to his home at the Father's side. "Eternal life is knowing you, the only true God," the man-God prays, "and Jesus Christ, whom you have sent." Reunion in heaven is what the Son asks now that his task is done.

The Father must hear his pleas for these apostles so newly consecrated. "I am not praying for the world, but for those whom you have entrusted to me; they belong to you, as all I have is yours, and all you have is mine; and in them my glory is achieved." The divine audacity of it! Jesus is telling the Father he must love the little band because they are one with the Son he loves. "Holy Father, keep them true to your name, your gift to me, that they may be one, as we are one. As long as I was with them, it was for me to keep them true . . . and I have watched over them." These apostles must stay in the world, for their Master has sent them out to continue his own work. What he asks of the Father is that he "should keep them clear of what is evil. They do not belong to the world, as I, too, do not belong to the world," cries the Lord; Father, "keep them holy, then, through your word; it is your word that is truth. I dedicate myself for their sakes."

The love Jesus desires to see burning in apostolic hearts abides no mediocrity. Its greatest enemy the Lord asks his Father to check, keeping his eleven clear of the world's contagion. Sin is the disrupter of oneness between him and his chosen. If our Lord so fears its effect on us, how clearly must we regard sin as the hateful despoiler of our friendship with him.

At this final moment of tranquility the Lord looks through time to us, to "those who are to find faith in me through [the apostles'] word." For us, too, Christ's prayer is for unity, "that they may all be one. . . . I have given them the privilege which you gave to me, that they should all be one, as we are one;

that while you are in me, I may be in them, and so they may be perfectly made one."

We are to be as truly intimates of God as the eleven. This divine friendship must produce in us the unity among ourselves and with God that will "let the world know," Jesus pleads with his Father, "that it is you who have sent me, and that you have bestowed your love upon them, as you have bestowed it upon me."

As the Master returns, almost obsessively, to the theme of unity, it should finally become clear to us that it is of the utmost importance. Not only the fruit of love—for all love seeks union with its object—it is the very sign that love has reached perfection. It is so difficult of achievement precisely because it can be only the fruit of love. And the term of our unity is eternal oneness with God. We see the end of this passionate appeal as the Master affirms, "This, Father, is my desire, that all those whom you have entrusted to me may be with me where I am, so as to see my glory." It is for our salvation, for the rescue of his friends, that our Lord is pleading. All, the Redeemer closes, so "that the love you have bestowed upon me may dwell in them, and I, too, may dwell in them."

Man has overheard the divine offertory to the sacrifice. Before the Master descends to the struggle and becomes dumb as the lamb before its shearer, he has dedicated in word what he must do in deed on the morrow. It is done to bring the unity love forms, and the love that is to do this, in Christ and in us, is a divine love alive in mortal men.

IT WILL BECOME IMPOSSIBLE TO CLAIM THAT THE MASTER DID NOT TOTALLY UNDERSTAND THE DIFFICULTIES SUPERNATURAL LOVE WILL ENCOUNTER IN THE WORLD. The grotesque sight of mankind rearing to crush Jesus stains this Friday for all time. Yet not so thoroughly learned is the truth that the Lord fully encountered, not just external strife, but all the difficult agonies God's love undergoes within man's nature. It would be cruel, indeed, were the Master to have painted his piercingly beautiful portrait of God's life-in-us so ideally that it would ignore man's inner turmoil. The objection that Christ, overlooking human limitations, gave us a dream-vision that forgot reality is fully countered by the experience he must undergo in Gethsemane's garden. Sin excepted, he *is* like us in all things.

What happens there in the dead of night? He has separated himself from the apostles. Only the witnesses of his glory at the transfiguration are to view it in reverse; then the Lord's divinity radiated his humanity, here it almost seems to desert him.

The glowing, already victorious, composure of the suppertime is stripped from him. God the Father has retracted from the human nature all awareness of what had been the man Jesus' greatest joy, knowing the divine nature was his. The Master feels this inner mastery slide away. He is profoundly unnerved, bewildered and, in his human senses, deeply frightened by this internal change. He is on the verge, he may well have felt, of losing control of himself.

Into this torment come the vision of his suffering to come, so totally excruciating, the vision of how useless his redemption will become for the many souls who will spurn or squander its merit, and the ultimate horror of visualizing the whole filth and meanness of sin descending upon him for him to carry as a victim. This immense load of grief forces his human sensibilities to scream in revolt against what lies ahead. Gripped in fearsome, shuddering emotion his body weeps blood. "My soul," he tells the apostles, "is ready to die with sorrow."

His first prayer that the Father spare him and take away

the cup of sorrow before him becomes finally, "My Father, if this may not pass me by, but I must drink it, then your will be done!" The awful struggle produces the great submission. The great act of free obedience is evoked that cancels Adam's disobedience. Stripped of all composure and cast into abysmal dejection, there still remains deep within him only the pure small voice of his love for his Father. It is the only voice that can calm this storm.

It is man, truly a man like us, who loves divinely here despite every sort of inner rage. In no way concealed is the agonizing stretch of human powers against the divine will. This is a contest that will be repeated in every human being possessed of divine life—may God's mercy preserve us from facing it in such intensity! The lesson, however, is unmistakably clear: Jesus knows and experiences what it is to have divine life truly within humanity's weakness. The difficulty is recognized; it is not suppressed as evil; yet the infinite power of God's love can lead it to the full internal gift of self that reaches conformity to God's will.

We have been exposed to sight of the complete reality of Christ's doctrine on charity. An ultimate stress test has been enacted before us. No one of us, as we are put to the trials God may put upon us, need ever fear that God's love in us has a breaking point.

It is just as obvious that every one of us will be tested so on how deep is our adherence to the divine life inserted in our souls. It is inherently necessary that we prove we value it above all else, even life itself.

THE FINAL YES HAS BEEN SPOKEN. Intruding into the garden comes noise of an approaching mob. A crowd bristling with weapons looms in the night. Lanterns and torches glint unnecessarily in the full moonlight; the tense mutter of war is behind every bush.

Jesus, who will regard no son so prodigal as beyond return, greets the man of the hour as "My friend!" But Judas stings him with his kiss of death, sure identification in the semi-darkness. The Master is seized; "darkness has its will." The shepherd struck, the flock scatters uncomprehending, fleeing with the swiftness of fear.

We have come full circle. The Judas who left the feast of the new Passover has returned. We are again in the clutches of a human race maddened against love.

But what has come between? In the peace that has intervened the Father's beloved Son has unveiled God's supreme message on charity. He has explained and enacted "the uttermost proof of his love." How much it will cost him the rest of this day will show.

What has been revealed by Jesus? With tender divine love we have heard him say: "I have bestowed my love upon you, just as my Father has bestowed his love upon me; live on, then, in my love." We have heard with wonder his command: "You are to love one another; that your love for one another is to be like the love I have borne you."

Knowing these mysteries, we must live on, then, in his love.

11 LOVE

The Last Day

WITH HURRICANE FORCE THE STORM IS UPON US. All the events and personages of the passion rush by, caught up in the wild winds of Good Friday. It is the day of confusion, the day of decision, the day of bitter tragedy and harsh glory, the day the Old Testament fell, the day when history reached its fulfillment.

Never will Peter forget it, for he faltered. His courage ebbs more slowly than that of the rest of the apostles and he rashly loiters outside the courtroom where the Master is being tried. The flock of servants there, with a portress in the lead, sense his fear and pursue Peter like a pack of yapping dogs. They badger big Peter into three frightened denials of his Lord. Thunderstruck by his disloyalty the prince of the apostles leaves our records of Good Friday weeping tears of shame. It is, however, a shame only true love could feel. And such was Peter's love for Jesus that this moment's failure would grieve him always.

Because of his abject failure, Judas, unlike the rock, shatters. Desperately he flings the thirty pieces of silver back into the temple, but he knows that this cannot undo what he has done. Helpless without the love that saves Peter, Judas concludes that he is beyond forgiveness. Reaching the end of his rope, he betrays even his own soul.

Cast with the biggest speaking parts are Caiaphas and Pilate. Before he is done Caiaphas has shrieked out words that blight this page of Israel's history, "We have no king but Caesar!" His hatred of Jesus overcomes all scruples. With bile and cunning Caiaphas engineers death for the Master.

Pilate's pathetic effort to free Jesus crumbles under attack. He senses the historic moment and, with alarm, the uncanny dignity of Jesus. These intuitions raise Pilate to his full stature as a judge but it is a dignity he is too personally weak to maintain. He is an arch though perceptive weakling.

Herod merely runs along and across the stage like the fool he claims Christ to be.

Ever present throughout this maelstrom of wickedness are the torturers. They are faceless. With fierce savagery they smash Jesus across the face, spit on him, outrage his honor in every way. Some vile delight seems to possess them as they flay their captive with scourges, push down into his head that spikey helmet of thorns, and then prance and fawn about him mockingly. This savage cruelty fills every hour until strangely it seems to mitigate as the professional rite of crucifixion begins.

The evangelists have drawn a discreet veil over the vicious agonies of the Lord. Most likely they felt powerless to describe them. Yet the gospels do give us a richly detailed account of this monstrous day, an account perhaps too richly detailed. It is too easy to let our mind follow with fascination the collapse of Pilate or the increasing desperation of Caiaphas. Distracted by dice and titleboards, bloodmoney and Barabbas, we can almost neglect that passive mute figure at the center of this horror.

Surrounded by all these howling tensions, Jesus stands bowed in the eye of the hurricane. Battered by flail and insult the Master silently absorbs every punishment. He is giving the "uttermost proof of his love."

It is to him we must attend. "Ecce Homo!" "Look, this is the Lamb of God who takes away the sin of the world."

The composure that envelops Jesus is not that of one who is insensible to torment. He is hurt, hurt by infidelity and contempt, by every lash and every thorn. Nor is he stoically enduring this suffering because it is unavoidable. More than making no effort to avoid its onslaught, the Lord has concentrated his whole being on absorbing all of it. He is utterly bent on making it most precious.

Useless and hateful in itself, suffering, without faith, is a curse. Yet we are witnessing the Master transform it into something valuable beyond measure. He is making all his anguish and agony into a gift to his Father.

It is a gift most personal. Suffering strips away selfishness with its knife if it is accepted as Jesus accepts it, and leaves the essence scraped of all detail. One cannot suffer casually; it touches our very being. And so to give it as a gift is to give what is most representative of self-donation. That is to say that Jesus gives what costs most. It is a gift only love can give.

He is a victim, and he embraces this victimhood as a prize. Already the priestly dedication of this sacrifice has directed it to his Father. The son is now amassing the treasure he would bring his Father. It is, above all, love's act. Useless and hateful in itself, suffering becomes the mysterious and glorious tool of love. Out of such bitter clay is formed mankind's most perfect offering to God. As we must never tire of loving God, we must never get tired of suffering.

Humility, we have said, does not exist fully until one finds that nothing is humiliating. It is love that accomplishes this, that renders us unconscious of what the gift costs. The aims of love overcome misgiving and self-concern. Suffering is not resisted but chosen by Christ. Jesus takes hold of it. With all the strength of his soul and body the Lord commits himself to the cross and all its heinous preliminaries. Suffering's ugliness is transfigured—not becoming any less suffering or any less ugly—because of why and how it is suffered.

"See, here is the man!" Pilate says to us, and what do we see? Within the bent form of a man scarred by suffering and trembling with pain we must see Jesus fiercely loving his Father with an infinite and most human love. He is teaching us, while we are in this painful world, how it is that we are to love.

JESUS IS THE OBJECT, THE VICTIM, OF MANKIND'S GREATEST SIN. Cruelty is all about him, yet of deeper injury are the scathing repudiations of his mission from the Father and of the holy heritage of Israel. Infernal hatred incites to fury and to sacrilege. All the sin of the world masses to fall on its Master. The horrendous cost of this Jesus strains to compensate with the rending cost of his love.

At every turn of the road, as again and again he collapses beneath the timber of his cross, as he bears the sneers of the Pharisees, as he endures the blinding bite of nail grinding through wrist and ankle, as he suffers the dreadful wrench and thud of his cross raising and then jolting into its socket, throughout each agony his lips mumble one incredible prayer: "Father, forgive them; they do not know what it is they are doing!"

Startling, unbelievable love that pleads for pardon, not God's curse. Forgiveness for persecutors, love for enemies—these are more than abstract attitudes of virtue now. The depths of our Master's love challenge us. No bitterness rears;

indeed, Jesus seems to forget entirely that we are not worthy at all, most of all at this moment. Clearly, no matter what we do, he cannot be disillusioned over us. Love accomplishes this blindness; to limit or retract his love is unthinkable, for Jesus loves us and has committed himself for us without limit. His passion is "for us and for our salvation."

True love is unfalteringly in favor of someone; it takes sides. Numbered among us, bone of our bone, Jesus takes our side, pleads our cause with his Father. This perfect gift he gives to the Father, this infinite sacrifice, is given in our name, for us. Abandoned to a cross by man, the Lord abandons himself for us. Ever our advocate, our intercessor, he begs, "Father, forgive them; they do not know what it is they are doing."

Naked now is the raw core of Christ's love; it is for us and as one of us that he is dying. His is a Savior's love, a ransoming, redemptive love, and "by his bruises are we healed." Yet, is this to say that his love is for this purpose? Or does love just love because it must? Does Jesus love us in order to save us? No; because he loves us, he saves us; wanting us, he takes us with him. We are loved salvifically because that is the full reach of the love Jesus will not limit in any way.

Love demands such a giving of self, an expenditure which so fully takes us out of ourselves that it becomes normal and logical to die in order to give life. All the same we would doubtless regard it as understandable and pardonable had our Lord hardly been able to turn his thoughts beyond his own excruciating anguish. Yet he does not enclose himself from us for a moment; he is dying for us.

How, then, does he treat the common criminal who speaks to him from the next cross? As his neighbor—as indeed this good thief is—and as his friend. Jesus immediately accepts equal stature with this criminal and shares with him all he has.

The Savior loves him: "This day you shall be with me in paradise." All his pain is no obstacle to his giving full attention to this criminal; there is no trace of condescension. Egotism would have made this impossible, but the love of Christ has shot far beyond egotism.

Jesus is not dying for his little band of followers alone. His redemption is universal because his love is universal. Apostles, disciples and holy women stand in the foreground, to be sure, yet just as present to the Lord are publicans and thieves, harlots and rulers—in short, rich or poor, all the wretched and unloved in the world. How mistaken about his Master's love was Judas! The only exclusion from it is self-imposed.

At this climactic moment we are vividly shown that love is more than a singular relationship to one object. Christian love must become an attitude, an orientation of character turned towards all lovingly. To love just one person and be indifferent to the rest of his fellowmen is, more likely than not, merely to exhibit an enlarged egotism. Unbounded love is our vocation; the only check on it is on its fruitfulness. This is to say that our love can be refused or ignored, but even that places no restraint on our continuing to love. It was so with our loving Savior.

FOR THE FIRST TIME SINCE HER SON'S OPENING MIRACLE AT CANA THE GOSPELS TELL US THAT THE MOTHER OF JESUS IS THERE. It is her hour as it is the "hour of Jesus." For so long she has been reserved for this peak moment of his life and work. All the help and all the cooperation she has desired to give her son—and been prevented from offering him—is to be concentrated here in the greatest moment of need. The collaboration denied her before pales in comparison with her opportunity now. Saved until last, like the best wine of Cana, is this heart-rending display of her love.

It is common to motherhood to seek, while hovering over a child ill or hurt, to make his suffering her own. Indeed, the mother's vicarious compassion can often seem more agonizing than that of her child. Unique mother that she was, this instinct to suffer with (and almost as if in place of) her son was eminently evident in Mary. She wished it were she in his stead and sought to absorb all his pain herself.

The passion he suffered she suffered by compassion. No one was so uniquely equipped to share and understand his travail. Every heaving throb of his heart was echoed in hers. Gifted so wondrously by providence, Mary learned totally the essential Christian lesson: she was one with him; and one with him as no one else but his mother could be. Here, then, occurred this mystery's climax: so closely knit, they are one victim. This is motherhood in triumph.

She had assented to this moment obscurely when first the angel came so long ago, and throughout the years she had nurtured this fiat to immense maturity. Profoundest faith sustains her act of sacrificial love. As he spends himself, so does she spend. In one act she is losing her God and her son, yet she permits this willingly, even gladly we dare to say, so dear is his work to his Father. It is so, then, that together they recreate the human race through sacrifice, his absolutely complete and hers perfect, too, and human.

Her offering love is so full of God that with our narrowed eyes we cannot see it all, yet blinded now we see God's glory more than just enough to fall and gasp amen.

What God has joined together, this mother and this son, death is soon to put asunder. Looking down on his mother, beloved beyond all other creatures, Jesus speaks his tender and compelling farewell. John the apostle is there. Is he there, and not gone with his fellow apostles, because Mary took him by the hand? Already she had his Church in hand.

Words, plain words, are spoken that may seem plain to others but not to these hearers united in his love. "Woman, this is your son. This is your mother."

Dying for us Jesus leaves us his whole treasure as inheritance, and on earth he treasures nothing or no one as Mary. She is not simply conferred into someone's care; she is to mother. Her faith and her love are sent to full scope; she is to love every one of his as she has loved him. She is to be mother of his brethren and his work, for she loves her son Jesus as he is, as not just hers alone. Mary accepts mankind substituted for her divine son, a whole multitude for the only-begotten, motherhood manifold.

In her John gains a mother for us all. "Behold," Mary sang out years before, "from this day forward all generations will count me blessed!"

ONCE WE BEGIN TO COMPREHEND THE LOVE OF MARY, AND THAT OF JOHN OR THE MAGDALEN, WE SEE THAT IT CANNOT BE SAID THAT JESUS WAS ALONE ON CALVARY. This unity of love we must observe with more than admiration, with imitation. Uniquely divine in Christ, this love is not exclusively Christ's as man. With Mary, John and the others, we are called to live this love. With her and all who are one with her son, we are drawn into this spectacle for we, too, are to love "as he has loved us." Brushing aside the flimsy barriers of time, Mary takes our hands in hers, as she does John's, to introduce us into this mystery at the very heart of man's history. We have each parts to play; we do not come only to watch. To receive we must give, and it is ourselves we must give. Height of privilege! Our Savior not only shares his love with us, but lets us give our share to his. So utter is our Master's union with mankind that he would have us not miss this share in the earning of our salvation. We are in no way dissociated from Jesus, savior, priest and victim for us all.

A desire to share our Savior's suffering must inflame us all. Who has not wished with secret ardor that Simon of Cyrene might have been himself? Or dreamed of finding oneself as close to the cross as Mary Magdalen? All the same there remains the frank internal reminder, such is our soft-boned weakness and lack of love, that all this is impossible for us. Honestly we must admit that we would have been cowering among the apostles, at best.

And so it is, unless Jesus infuses into us his immense power to love. That is exactly, we recall, what charity is: his love to love with, his strength to be strong with, his courage in giving become our own. So done, the passion of Jesus continues in us, and "in us his glory is achieved!" Nothing less than this is the role of those who are called to be one with Jesus the Savior.

To recoil from giving ourselves up to the cross completely, from "taking hold" of it, is to limit love. Have no illusions over what God will ask from us. First to accept and endure the crosses that mark our lives like his and, then, one with him, to come to love them. Complete faith in the love he shares, and that alone, can dissolve the impossibility within us. Here, though, we have the superlative example of Mary and the others like ourselves to urge us on. We will never be alone.

So infinitely precious is God's redemptive love that once possessed it must be shared with all. Perfect contact between Calvary and our moment in time is achieved in us. But more, this love becomes in us the connective between then and now for all around. Loving all as he loves, we can share in others' salvation, for it is through us, then, that they are loved with the Savior's love. This is the vocation of the Christian, of other Christs large and small.

There is possible no subtraction of self, no partial giving, if we would impart the whole Christ. It is our own sufferings as well as our Lord's that we offer up against all the misery and anxiety and weakness of the world. Our hardships and pain are paltry indeed, it is true, yet they are all-powerful if they are in contact with the cross of Jesus. Then his accomplishment gleams in us and—such is God's majestic plan—his life and love can penetrate into our world's immense distress.

This is what love does; it makes death give life.

OUR EYES MUST ALWAYS BE ON JESUS CRUCIFIED, FOR HE IS OUR SALVATION AND OUR WHOLE SUPPORT. All ages' sin and grief bear down on him. This horrid avalanche of evil the Master accepts as if it were his own; he is substitute for every one of us. He is agonized and mute with guilt.

Love grapples with this burden beyond imagining. Ever just short of that short-circuit of the nerves that would mercifully bring unconsciousness, Jesus offers his heart's life to his Father in atonement. He gives the "uttermost proof of his love" for us.

Other men's heads fall in death; Jesus bows his head. Other men have their lives taken from them; our Savior yields up his spirit voluntarily. Breathing out his human life in filial abandonment, the prodigal son, having spent all his substance, returns to his Father. For this ultimate sacrifice he had come into the world. Then there is a rupture, self-willed, of this sacred heart in a rapture of love. And Christ, the Jesus, is dead.

We stand beneath this saving cross of Jesus. Our blessed mother is there with all the saints. With aching hearts we realize the overwhelming depths of love we are invited to share. "He is not worthy of me," this crucified lover has pronounced, "that does not take up his cross and follow me."

It is true that living a life of love is the only completely satisfying existence in this world. This love Jesus offers to us and for us transcends heaven and earth. Brilliant with mystery though it is and shot through with self-sacrifice, we must embrace and love the cross with our entire heart and soul.

Nothing less will do, for there is a whole race of men to be loved and saved. It is like living in a hurricane's eye yet we must, for we know now that our Lord declares it to be essential: "He is not worthy of me, that does not take up his cross and follow me."

Such is the scope and the cost and the glory compressed into that one direction our Savior leaves us: "You are to love one another *as I have loved you.*"

12 HOPE

The Risen Lord

To ask what the apostles expected as Good Friday shuddered to a close is to ask an impossible question. How could anyone think beyond what they had witnessed? It was unspeakable, incredible tragedy. The way is closed; the truth obliterated; the life is dead.

Is there any room for hope? They could hardly have wondered, so glutted were their souls with sorrow. Yet, beneath this sea of sadness, underneath the ache of horror at death and burial, there was an ultimate, inarticulate ocean-bed. Faith was still there. Only a Sabbath rest could let it clarify.

With the dawning of the Easter morning sun a resplendent angel arrives at the tomb of Jesus to exhibit the resurrection as accomplished. He rolls back the stone door and sits almost mockingly on it. It guards only an empty tomb for, the angel announces, "He is risen, he is not here!"

Before she hears this announcement Mary Magdalen is already running wildly to Peter with the fearsome news that the Master's grave has been violated. And Easter morning's hectic parade to the tomb begins.

159

The rest of the women wander off dazed by the angel's message while Peter and John race towards the sepulchre. John's youth tells in this race into mystery yet, in deference to Peter's chiefly role, he waits so that he can follow. Quickly the evidence is viewed and found bewildering. The Lord's burial clothes lie there neatly piled; could the body have left unwrapped? Strangely excited, the two leave "full of surmise." At least some space was clearing in their souls that would leave room for the possibilities of God.

The Magdalen then returns to search for the stolen corpse. So bereft is she that her tears blind her. Mistaking the risen Jesus for a gardener she almost incoherently attacks him with questions. Then hearing her Lord call her by name she falls in instant, overwhelming recognition at his feet. It was her place so often before. Indeed if the eleven form the human containers, the alabaster box-sides, of the paschal mystery to be carried through time and space, it is Mary Magdalen at the risen Christ's feet that exhibits the perfume within that must permeate history. It will always be the highest function of the Church to fall at the feet of Jesus and cry "Master!"

The Master has changed. He is exalted yet still tender; exultant yet sober. Risen, his relationship with his brethren will rise also. Mary must not cling to him but hurry to the eleven with her good news.

Sorrow afflicts a woman's heart when she loses her beloved; men generally become perplexed in mind when viewing their shattered fortunes. To a stranger they meet on the road to Emmaus two disciples pour out their tragic tale. They conclude their sad account to the unrecognized Master with heavy word: "For ourselves, we had hoped that it was he who was to deliver Israel."

What kind of hope was this? Did they mean they thought

that Jesus had had a "chance" of becoming the Savior? How sure had their hope been if so soon it seemed already a chance lost?

No, the true reason for hope has not changed. The stranger turns on the two startled disciples: "Too slow of wit, too dull of heart, to believe all those sayings of the prophets! Was it not to be expected that the Christ should undergo these sufferings, and enter so into his glory?" The passion is the purchase-price of even greater glory. And ranging through God's previews of the Savior in holy writ, prophecy after prophecy fell into fulfillment.

Imagine the lucky two gradually reviving, their faith refurbished, their hope kindled to a blaze. They insist that this stranger sup with them. He accepts their invitation to be their guest but immediately becomes their host, for he breaks bread and they knew then that the stranger was himself the bread come down from heaven, given for the life of the world.

This exquisite episode does not conclude when the Master vanishes. We are further treated to a precious sight of the risen one's effect. "Were not our hearts burning within us when he spoke to us on the road, and when he made the scriptures plain to us?" they cried out with joy. Joy was their response to his presence. Hope had returned and with flaming radiance! Over and over again they must have repeated this to each other as they hastened back towards Jerusalem, their supper forgotten.

Their news was not as fresh as they thought; the Lord had also appeared to Peter. As yet there was no joyful mood there to match their own new confidence. All the rumors and hectic investigations of this Sunday had not lifted the gray blanket of doubt. Almost afraid to hope, the apostles barred the doors to the upper room to meet and weigh Easter's happenings.

They are deep in these discussions when suddenly the risen Jesus stands in their midst. "Peace be upon you," he greets them. And, the gospels tell us, "they cowered down, full of terror, thinking that they were seeing an apparition." Perhaps nothing frightened them so much as the suddenness of his arrival in spite of the doors they had bolted so carefully. "What!" says the Lord, "are you dismayed?" Aren't you glad to see me? Look at me, touch me, test whether I am ghost or not. And, patient with their amazement, the Master eats a piece of roast fish, for no spectre eats. "You will see me again and your hearts will rejoice," he had said on Thursday in this room. Now they were overjoyed; in fact, excess of joy and surprise made them wonder if it were not all too good to be true. They were at once awed, elated and overwhelmed.

After they had settled down a bit Jesus called them to attention solemnly: "Peace be upon you. I came upon an errand from my Father," he announces, "and now I am sending you out in my turn." Jesus breathes on them, God's speechless Spirit issuing upon them as a divine sigh of life-conferral; "Receive the Holy Spirit." As the Father breathed human life into Adam, spiritual life comes now into Christ's body the Church. Judiciously the apostles are to undo what Christ has undone: sin itself. "When you forgive men's sins, they are forgiven," the Master tells them, completing his ordination of Thursday past. Then they had received power over his sacramental body; now it is power over his mystical body he confers. His kingdom must have "all authority in heaven and earth" as does its Master.

If before this Easter experience the apostles had primarily viewed the humanity of Jesus and his divinity only as it were in brilliant, broken flashes, all is changed now. Now with the risen Lord in their midst it is his divinity that is at the center of their faith and ever will it so remain. Their conception of his humanity is now, instead, to be regulated by his divinity. To their idea of Jesus, therefore, the Easter experience brought this significant, deepening clarification. This Lord of theirs truly is from God the Father's side. The resplendent risen Master in their midst makes this certainty present, evident and unforgettable.

This reality of God appears before their eyes as something entirely transcendent, a live mystery, no puzzle distant and abstract. Magnetically impressed, their minds and hearts are drawn from the earth and its powers to their heavenly Lord and the might of his resurrection. The world of space and time sinks out of the first ranks of reality. The center of gravity shifts from earth to heaven. And it is in this new view that the apostles see the kingdom of God and their immense role. Christ's is indeed a kingdom "not of this world"—so often this is said sadly, as if to excuse him, as if it lessens him!—yet now the reality of his transcendent kingship shines in him. That kingdom, so shyly and almost unnoticeably putting out its roots in Palestine's soil, now stands clear in the true grandeur of its risen Master. This kingdom, above and beyond this world, is all the same within us now. And with his masterful power these eleven men are to be his agents, his "dispensers of the mysteries of God."

We must not pass over the huge internal change that the resurrection effects within Christ's band of followers. Their insights and values are overturned and expanded. They suddenly know in every recess of their beings that it is man's fate not to die but to live, and live resurrected. The Lord Jesus is becoming timeless to the apostles. They sense the new and pervading permanence of his presence, and its power. Always will they preach of him as present, powerful, reigning and transforming—never as past.

The resurrection inaugurates a new life of faith, hope and

charity. In its blinding light all that precedes appears as preparation. From Easter on life is new.

Indeed, when a man turns his life towards the ultimate center which is God, allowing strength and divine love to pour into his innermost being, then his life grows and its branches tower into eternity. It is hope that heaves aside all the natural weight of man and uncoils the springing of the soul towards God. And it is precisely the risen Jesus that gives us such truly supernatural hope, just as he set it to singing in the souls of his apostles and burning in the hearts of his companions on the road to Emmaus. Hope is our response to the cosmic remove of the center of gravity from our earth's core to heaven. And it is possible because heaven, in the person of Christ risen, is brought back to earth. Hope, radiant, joyful and loaded with eternal promise, is above all the Easter virtue. One with the risen one we come to life in him: this is the whole of our hopes and dreams!

Hope recognizes and responds to this vital possibility. It leaps up with unshakeable confidence because it is God almighty who invites and exercises his almighty power. It is for faith to see and certify this vista, but it is for hope to make it real and reachable for each of us. This is the essence of the change we see in the apostles. Overwhelmed by the victorious presence of their risen Lord, they respond each with a new concentration of being, a mighty focussing of intent. They are changed men, and this is hope's doing.

WHAT IS TO BE SAID OF THE APOSTLE'S FAITH NOW THAT EASTER HAS LIT THEM WITH NEW LIFE? Hope springs so high from faith's new vitality. Hope is transfigured because faith is. In those school-room days, when it was mainly the Master's humanity that the disciples saw, their faith was frail. It was an all too human accomplishment that beat back doubt and fear with constant struggle. Easter brings an immediate experience of the majesty and might of God. This supernatural sight banishes doubt; faith, so touched by radiant grace, is transformed into a certainty as absolute as God.

Man has a part to play here. Notice that the risen Lord appears only to the faithful, to the initiated, to those prepared. This transformation can occur only in hearts already lifted towards him, only where men's minds keep watch in simple and humble awareness of their own need for the powers of redemption that issue forth from the figure of Christ. Somewhat apart from the explosive events of the great Sunday the gospels give us an undistracted view of faith leaping to fulness in the case of the apostle Thomas.

Perhaps it was the wild confusion of Easter day—and all that female emotion—that set Thomas' teeth on edge. Someone has to keep his head, he must have thought. Faced later with the high spirits of his brethren and their high tales of the visit he had missed, he must have hardened in his role of devil's advocate. But he is mistaken. It is not the touching of his Master's wounds that will convince him; grace's touch is what he lacks.

The resurrection is a mystery that God's grace unlocks to us, a mystery of faith. Confronted by grace, Thomas falls and proves he was prepared for this moment by blurting out the most exalted acclamation of Jesus in the gospels: "You are my Lord and my God!" The Christ of glory draws from him the simplest, truest and grandest act of faith. Happy indeed are those whose belief is beyond sight and its demand for proof, yet happy too is Thomas for he as well is now full of reasons for hope. He is joined again to his Master and his friends at this new and joyous height. His Lord and God has taken him in hand.

From this high vantage point so many other truths gradu-

ally and finally fall into place. One of these certainly was—
the stumbling block for so many—that suffering is the necessary means of reaching the Father. The gospels are silent as to
the full extent of the risen Lord's teaching; we see it recorded
rather in the first preaching of his hearers. For the eleven the
blissful certainty of their own resurrection became the heart
of their long-range hopes. This was not merely a matter of
their own souls entering finally into heaven's bliss. It was
rather the great new message of Christian hope, that eternal
life is essentially resurrection, the resurrection and new creation of man that they were to proclaim to all. All can come to
life in Jesus risen.

This is the joy that the kingdom possesses within its gates.
Deep reverberations of joy rumble through creation now that
this perfect happiness can be hoped for, because it is attain-
able really through God's masterful aid. "My Lord and my
God," seen fully in faith, gives substance to this brilliant hope.
So glorious is God's Easter gift of hope!

Our next record of Christ's doings tells of his touching
reunion with the apostles in their Galilee homeland. Warmly
are we exposed to two further aspects of Christian hope.

God's love united with hope and faith make perfect partners. With every delicate touch of the lakeside scene the risen
Lord shows that his love for them is as close as ever. As his
fishers clamber ashore with the prize catch he gave them, they
find the Master has a fire going and breakfast on the way. He
is not too exalted to be their servant still.

"And when they had eaten, Jesus said to Simon Peter,
'Simon, son of John, do you care for me more than these others?'
'Yes, Lord, you know well that I love you,' " comes Peter's
shamed answer. What is the Master doing as he repeats this
awkward question once more and then again? He is undoing

the damage of Peter's triple denial and more. With penetrating love he is showing us the way God forgives. His pardon makes it possible for us to love him better. And it is a changed Peter who is purified and, for once, avoids the pitfall of over-protesting.

Hope has one built-in limitation that it is for charity to overcome. By its very notion hope is individual, involving directly only my own or your own personal salvation. Christian love dilates hope beyond itself. In this partnership the borders of hope broaden as wide as charity reaches. It becomes a community virtue, not to be isolated only in oneself.

In this climate Peter can see hope and love both in that simple, awesome conferral of authority Jesus makes: "Feed my sheep." The promised primacy is awarded, but in the gentle loving guise of a shepherd's staff, for it is a task that calls for a shepherd's love. As a further gift to Peter the Lord promises that he will be asked to die for his Master, that the full extent of sacrificial love will be called for. Peter, at last, is to be at the crucifixion. Our Lord's invitation — "Follow Me!" — is complete.

Although it is correct that the true nature of hope renders despair impossible, it is all too easy to make an opposite mistake. Anyone who might see hope as a release from care and responsibility, as some sort of escape into an immediate and blissful dream-world, has not recognized hope. Now is a time of grace, not yet a time for glory. The cross has not been removed. Under hope's gaze the Christian life remains a warfare, but a war with total victory in sight.

Hope grants a sure and basic confidence which, all the same, is fringed with uncertainty. A serene and quiet expectation without danger is foreign to hope, for it is the virtue of hope to strain and struggle towards its goal. Peter, loaded with gigantic responsibilities, cannot forget his own frailty. There is no question as to whether God will lend his strength. Still, hope certainly includes a grave awareness of the caution with which we must regard ourselves. Prudence and purity of heart must be our guardians against presumption.

However arduous, the cross is now a glorious cross. Hope enables us to see through all of time's trials and sufferings, and bear them with glorious patience. This is not to say that we should look beyond our agonies in this world; rather, we can see within all the privations and hardships of this life, with the insight of hope, the necessary and glorious path to resurrection. Hope draws triumph from tribulation, joy from suffering, for we are following Jesus who has destroyed death.

Time enough for all this when the bridegroom is gone; right now Easter joy still rings in Israel's air. Undaunted by the immensities involved in the future before them, the apostles are yet overjoyed at the radiant presence of their beloved Master. This is a joy that will last but in a different, more internal manner. For just as through faith we share in God's truth, and through charity begin to love with God's love, it is God's joy that we start to enjoy through hope. This foretaste of God's happiness is hope's child. Feelings may come and go, but its joyous reality in us is placed down deep within where faith and love reside, down where God places the gifts he means to last. Every Christian cheats himself if he forgets or neglects this inner current of happiness that shines with divine assurance and might.

Indeed this confidence and this conviction is what confers on the whole message of Christ its mysterious, lilting exhilaration. His Gospel will always be good news because it is full of joyous, risen hope for every one of us, no matter if we be least or last or however lost.

LEAVING-TIME HAS COME. It is an index of the great new depth in the eleven that we discover them surrounding their Master on the mountaintop all bowed down in worship before him. The seed of eternal life has been planted and the eyes of Jesus are already on the harvest. "You, therefore," he commands them, "must go out all over the world, and preach the gospel to the whole of creation, making disciples of all nations." The mission is to be catholic; there is hope for all. The baptismal graces coming from Father, Son and Holy Spirit, graces of resurrection, must vivify all mankind, as his commandments must regulate them. It is a matter of life or death, and he is the resurrection and the life.

The eleven simple men the Lord leaves behind are become his plenipotentiary ambassadors, mighty givers of the goods of God, his creative witnesses. He does not leave them alone. His final words before he ascends are his solemn and total promise that they shall never be without him or without hope. "Behold I am with you all through the days that are coming, until the consummation of the world!"

He blesses them—such an enveloping, tender act. What blessings he leaves with us! Earth-bound, the eleven can follow him now only with their eyes until, gone in the clouds, Jesus begins to be visible only to the eyes of faith. Men of Galilee, announce the angels, looks earthwards now. Your Jesus will return and you must be ready to receive him with your work done.

And they bowed down to worship him
who is seated now at the right hand of God.

He who centuries ago was slain as a felon in an out-of-the-way corner of the world, today lives the same sublime life among us, in us, with us. He is more alive than all the living. Above all the needs of the present, above all the cramping limitations of human existence, above all the quarrels of states and nations, above the graves of our loves there still floats his figure in its gleaming whiteness. And we know that he alone is the real union of the living and the dead, that he alone is our eternal life. We see him more plainly than we do visible things. We love him more than we do any human being. We confess him no less sincerely than did the disciples in days gone by. For the truth is that every genuine Christian life proclaims, with an ever new voice in ringing tones, the fact to which the apostles once testified with their blood: "He is risen from the dead, of which we are witnesses!"

—Karl Adam (*Son of God*, p. 262)

RETREAT PRAYERS

Beginning a Conference:

Jesus,
You are the Son of the living God,
You have the words of eternal life,
You take away the sins of the world,
You are the bread of life,
    containing in yourself all delight.

Give me now the graces I need.
Quiet my soul to receive without distraction your message.
Grant me purity of heart,
    so that I will accept, love and act in simple unity
with you. Be in me.

and you,
Mary,
You who knew him so well,
You who absorbed all the graces he gave,
You who had him to yourself for thirty quiet years,
You, Mother, bring me to be your son. Amen.

173

After a Conference:

Almighty Father
I abandon myself to you.
Do with me whatever you wish.
For whatever you do with me
I thank you for it.

I am ready for anything—
I accept everything, so that
What you want may be done in me
And in all your handiwork.
I want nothing else, my God.

I lay my soul in your hands.
I give it to you, my God,
With all the love of my heart,
Trusting myself, without limit, to your care,
Because I love you so
That I need to give myself to you
With an infinite trust,
Because you are
                    My Father.

(Charles de Foucauld)